TO YOUR FIRST YEAR OF
LAW SCHOOL

TO YOUR FIRST YEAR OF
LAW SCHOOL

A Student-to-Student Handbook
from a Law School Survivor

JUSTIN SPIZMAN, J.D.

Adams Media
Avon, Massachusetts

Published by
Adams Media, an F+W Publications Company
57 Littlefield Street, Avon, MA 02322. U.S.A.
www.adamsmedia.com

ISBN 10: 1-59869-084-1
ISBN 13: 978-1-59869-084-2

Printed in Canada.

J I H G F E D C B A

Library of Congress Cataloging-in-Publication Data
Spizman, Justin.
The insider's guide to your first year of law school / Justin Spizman.
p. cm.
ISBN-13: 978-1-59869-084-2 (pbk.)
ISBN-10: 1-59869-084-1 (pbk.)
1. Law–United States–Study and teaching. 2. Law students–
United States–Handbooks, manuals, etc. I. Title.

KF283.S65 2007
340.071'173–dc22

This publication is designed to provide accurate and authoritative information with regard to the subject matter covered. It is sold with the understanding that the publisher is not engaged in rendering legal, accounting,
or other professional advice. If legal advice or other expert assistance is
required, the services of a competent professional person should be sought.
　—From a *Declaration of Principles* jointly adopted by a Committee of the
American Bar Association and a Committee of Publishers and Associations

Many of the designations used by manufacturers and sellers to distinguish
their product are claimed as trademarks. Where those designations appear
in this book and Adams Media was aware of a trademark claim, the designations have been printed with initial capital letters.

This book is available at quantity discounts for bulk purchases.
For information, please call 1-800-289-0963.

This book is dedicated to all those law students who came before me and those who will come after me. To those who came before me, thank you for your lessons, your stories, and your guidance. To those who come after me, use your predecessors' mistakes as lessons, their stories as inspiration, and their guidance as a way to save your butt when things get tough. Always remember, when you feel like there is no way out and failure is imminent, think of the most dimwitted attorney you have met and remember that he somehow survived his first year. If he did it, then so can you. Good luck and happy trails.

Table of Contents

CHAPTER ONE: **What to Expect in Your First Year**

CHAPTER TWO: **Preparing for the Cl-ass Kicking of Your Life**

CHAPTER SIX: Follow Through: Studying and Taking the Test

CHAPTER SEVEN: Legal Writing: What's the Difference and How Is It Done?

CHAPTER EIGHT: Distractions: The Good, the Bad, and the Necessary

CHAPTER NINE: **Go Forth, Young Scholar**

Acknowledgments

I would like to thank my family and friends for their support, guidance, and endless involvement in my life. Without you, this book would never have come to life. A special thanks to my mother, father, sister Ali, grandparents, and guardian angel Bettye Storne for inspiring me to write this book and supporting me along the way. You are the best cheering squad I could ever ask for. I would also like to extend a special thank-you to George H. Ross for his inspiring words and involvement in my book. Finally, I would like to thank my agent, John Willig, for his guidance and effort along every step of the book journey. Without him, this book would have never come to life.

The Insider's Guide to Your First Year of Law School is about learning from the mistakes and experiences of others, and I would like to thank all of my classmates, colleagues, mentors, professors, bosses, and attorneys for their additions to the book and their desire to help those who came after them. This book is a reflection of your teachings, and, for that, endless generations of 1Ls owe each of you a handshake.

Dear Future First-Year Law Student,

I wrote this book with someone just like you in mind. Perhaps you've just been accepted to law school or are currently navigating the application process. Not too long ago I was standing in your shoes. Curious, scared, nervous, and anxious were just a few of the thoughts rattling around in my head. When I finally received my acceptance to law school, I was elated. My family was overjoyed. While I was also a bit cautious about leaving my old life behind, I knew the most rewarding challenge of my life was just around the corner. I knew little about my journey ahead, but I figured I would learn the rules along the way.

To date, I have just finished—or should I say officially survived—my second year of law school. If I had only known then what I know now, I am confident that I would have gotten off to a running start rather than a steady crawl during my orientation as a 1L. And if I knew the "law school ropes," I could have transformed my first year from less stressful to more successful.

The term *1L* might sound innocent enough on the surface, but trust me it's a beast in itself. Once you become one, you are one of the lucky few allowed to enter the world of the justice system. Soon, you find yourself praying you make it through the first year's hurdles. In writing this book my goal is to tell you what it's really like, how to successfully prepare for it, and ultimately, how to succeed as a first-year law school student. You will learn from my failures and gain insight from my successes. In this book, I will chronicle the most stimulating and demanding events of my first year. After you read this book, you will be better prepared than other students could ever dream of being. You will even be ready to take on law school armed with knowledge from a 1L survivor.

Law school begins as one overwhelming assignment after another, but it doesn't have to be an impossible task. I am writing this book because I have experienced those challenges firsthand and now know the ins and outs that would have helped me along the way. In this book I will share with you exactly what you can expect from your first year in law school. The new language, the intense competition, the difficult material, and the Socratic method are all things I learned the hard way. I had to blaze my own trail, and only wish that I'd had a compass to help me navigate the way.

No previous experience, challenge, or schooling will totally prepare you for the obstacles ahead. But there are things you can do to ease the stress, get more accomplished, and learn how to get ahead. Law school is a unique animal that calls for unique training in order to tame it. This training is something that can be acquired if you use the right resources. While there are hundreds of helpful tools readily available at your fingertips, it is your responsibility and choice to locate these resources and effectively use them. I'll show and tell you how.

The purpose of this book is to teach you how to win at the wonderful game of law school. Yes, law school is a new and tough opportunity. There are rules (course materials), players (other students), and coaches (professors). Law school is a contact sport, and to succeed, you must know how to play the game. Even before Michael Jordan sunk his first "jumper" on the basketball court, he had to learn the rules of the game. In approaching the game from this pragmatic direction he left a permanent mark on the court and on the sport. While your skills and ability will improve as you manage the journey, this book can offer you the rules of the game before you start playing.

This is one of the hardest journeys you will ever make, so my best advice is to start with an advantage. Read this book and get the rules from an insider who has already been there and wishes he'd done that. Be ahead of the game and you will have a much better chance for 1L success. Take it from me. I'm now a graduate and survivor.

Justin Spizman

Although I have been practicing law for more than fifty years, I can remember my first year of law school like it was yesterday. At this point in my career, I have closed multimillion-dollar deals for Donald Trump, served as business adviser, legal counsel, and negotiator for the leading real estate owners and developers in New York City, authored two bestsellers, *Trump Style Negotiation* and *Trump Strategies for Real Estate,* and costarred in an extremely successful reality television show, *The Apprentice.* Based on my expertise in the art of negotiation, I served as a professor at NYU's School of Professional Studies and Continuing Education, teaching a course on negotiation.

My success had humble beginnings. It started in a crowded classroom at Brooklyn Law School. My wife worked to put me through law school and to this day I jokingly tell her that I think she got a pretty good return on her investment. I worked hard during my first year and did well, but there were many times when I felt frustrated, defeated, and overwhelmed. However, those feelings just made me push harder because I knew that the more difficult the task, the greater the reward.

When I began law school, there was little information out there concerning achieving success and learning the tricks of the trade. You went to law school, studied hard, and passed the BAR. That was the system, and I lived it. In retrospect, I wish that before I entered law school I had had the benefit of the experience and the trials and tribulations of someone who lived through it. Justin Spizman's book, *The Insider's Guide to Your First Year of Law School: A Student-to-Student Handbook from Law School Survivor,* is a great resource for incoming law students. If I'd had a book like this when I started my first year, I would have avoided plenty of needless headaches and aggravation.

You are extremely fortunate that a first-year survivor took the time to document his journey and share his insider's secrets to law school survival and success.

Enjoy your law school experience and keep this book by your side during the entire journey. I can promise you one thing: You're going to need all the seasoned help you can possibly get.

George H. Ross
Executive Vice President and Senior Counsel
The Trump Organization

AUGUST 23, 2003

My First Day

True story. Today was our first contracts class. The professor entered the room and walked firmly to the front of the class. He moved like a ghost, and as he approached the podium, he placed his books on the desk and introduced himself. "My name is Professor Roberts. Enough with the introductions—let's begin." A chuckle passed through the class. While I heard the laughs, all I thought was, "What the hell happened to syllabus day?" This was the big league. He then called attendance and dove right into the material. "Can anyone please define a contract?" No answer. "Fine, no volunteers. Mr. Smith, what is a contract? "An agreement between two people." "An agreement between two people for what? Who is sitting next to you?" "I don't know." "Well, she is your classmate. Introduce yourself and ask her name." He reluctantly agreed. "Her name is Ms. Jones. She is a first-year law student." "Thank you, Mr. Smith. I did not ask for her life story." Ms. Jones began to answer. She paused. Professor Roberts looked at her. She then continued talking, obviously fishing for the right answer. Roberts looked at her and said, "At what point did my silence make you feel justified in your endless babbling?" "I am sorry, sir." I sat there laughing at this comment, then I heard, "Mr. Spizman, what is so funny?" Damn. Busted. I sat forward, clutched my desk, and thought, what the hell have I gotten myself into?

1

Let the Game Begin

Welcome to my first law school experience. It was nerve-racking and a stronger dose of reality than I was ready to deal with. It felt like a bad hangover. Only minutes before this experience I was purchasing books, booting up my laptop to check my fantasy football team, and talking with my friends about our summer travels. Now these all seemed like distant memories. This was real. This was hard. This was ridiculous. This was law school. While my first experience in law school was less than inspiring, this does not always have to be the case. Fear does not always have to be the first experience you have on your first day of class. A little preparation can truly make all the difference. If that first student knew the definition of a contract, his life would have been much easier. Students make it so hard on themselves sometimes. It would have been so easy to know a simple definition of the course topic, but not a single student prepared for the easiest question we would be asked all semester. They say you only have one chance to make a first impression. This is all too familiar in law school. From the first day of class to the last interview before you enter the real world, first impressions play an enormous role. This chapter will help you prepare not only for the experience of your life, but also for the most important first impression you will ever make.

Orientation

As with most new environments, law schools offer an orientation program to acquaint new students with their surroundings. The time you spend in their law school's orientation program is essential to success as a first-year student. While this is not class, there may be assignments and required reading. Do the reading, attend orientation, and pay close attention. This time should be taken very seriously.

Orientation programs are generally scheduled the week before classes begin. This is advantageous, as the orientation material will be fresh in your mind when classes begin. Consider orientation as a taste of what's to come in the next three years. You will check in with orientation staffers and make sure your classes are in order, tuition is paid, and all registration details are finalized. Following this short process, you will be ushered into a large auditorium and will be the lucky recipients of words of encouragement and expectations from deans, teachers, and admissions staff. Finally, you will receive a tour of your new environment and will have the chance to ask second- and third-year students endless questions concerning the upcoming years. Orientation is the last protective barrier between law school students and their new course load. Therefore, when orientation comes to an end, reality sets in and playtime is officially over.

Orientation was an overwhelming experience. It is safe to say that you will hit the floor running. Professors, students, and administrators bombard you with endless amounts of information in an accelerated manner. I didn't know left from right when I walked out of the auditorium at the end of the day. I thought I had made a mistake. I was sure this was going to be the hardest experience of my life. Well, I was one for two as a prognosticator. My first year of law school was the hardest experience of my life, but I did not make a mistake. Remember, orientation is not supposed to be a scare tactic, but rather a guidance program. Take a deep breath, look around, and realize that you are not alone and everyone else in the auditorium is sharing your fears, concerns, and emotions.

Orientation is a time to nip the small headaches in the bud. There is no reason for you to be worried about your loans, parking, books, classroom assignments, lunch, or anything else on your first day of actual classes. Deal with all these small problems and issues during orientation. On your first day you should only be worried about the first impression you make and the materials for each class.

Most orientation programs last about a week. This will give you enough time on campus to take care of anything and everything you can think of. It is extremely frustrating to deal with problems concerning loans, class scheduling, or anything for that matter, over the phone. You are now in the lion's den. So if you have a problem, take this time and go talk to the kings of the jungle (professors, administrators, etc.).

Ways to Use Orientation to Your Advantage
- Purchase your books and supplements.
- Set up parking arrangements for each day of class.

- Make sure you have paid your tuition and are in good standing with your school.
- Make sure your class schedule is correct.
- Print out your schedule and locate all of your classrooms.
- Locate convenient spots to have lunch and grab snacks throughout the day.
- Introduce yourself to your classmates and professors.
- Register your computer and install the required programs the law school offers.
- Obtain a student identification card from the law school.

These are just a few steps you can take to reduce the chance of headaches, distractions, and mistakes on the first day of classes. You will have enough on your plate just dealing with the course materials. You don't need anything else to worry about.

Ways to Ensure a Successful Orientation

Come prepared: Don't take anything for granted. Bring paper, pens, and even your laptop so you can take notes, as you will be given a ton of information in a short period of time

Pay attention: While many of these orientation sessions may be long and, at times, a bit on the tedious side, pay attention and take good notes, because many of the questions you have coming into orientation will be answered while you are at orientation

Ask questions: This is a great opportunity to put many of your concerns to rest. You will be speaking directly with classmates, second- and third-year students, administrators, and teachers, all of whom have the answers to your tough questions. Use these resources and do not let this opportunity go to waste

Take notes: Whatever your preference, pen and paper or laptop, make sure you take notes throughout the entire orientation process. You will be presented with tons of new information, and the last thing you want is to forget everything you learned during the briefing process because you did not write it down.

Relax and enjoy: Do not freak out during orientation. Try not to get overwhelmed by all the information presented. You are not the first student to experience orientation and will certainly not be the last. Remember, you were accepted to law school because the administrator thought you could handle the curriculum. Relax, enjoy your last few days of freedom, and do not waste time being stressed or concerned this early in the journey.

The First Day

Merely days after orientation ends, law school classes begin. The first day of a law school is quite different from the first day of courses in college. The first day of law school is rarely referred to as "syllabus day." Generally, the professor begins outlining the course and discussing the court cases that most significantly shaped the law in that particular area of course study. Syllabus day becomes "syllabus five minutes." Within this first round of classes, you will helplessly look around and find little comfort in your new surroundings. The rooms are large, your classmates are blank-faced, and the all-knowing professor seems larger than life.

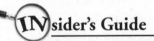 **sider's Guide**

Professor Pointer

Professor Doug Isenberg says, "Law school, especially the first—and most important—year, can be overwhelming, so the best thing anyone can do to prepare, and to keep from becoming overwhelmed, is to do as much advance work as possible and do everything practical to avoid falling behind. So, buy your first-year law books early and spend a lot of time preparing for the first week of class."

However, once time begins to pass, law school becomes less of a perplexing monster, and more of an unwelcoming in-law. It is true that few will ever find comfort in the hardships of life as a law student, but it is a means to an eventual end—a degree you are passionate about and finally, a payday. While the first few weeks may seem hopelessly challenging, you will find a bit of comfort when you fall into your daily routines.

So what does a typical day of law school feel like?
- You should begin your day by arriving at school thirty minutes before your first class of the day to review notes and case-briefs.
- Use the restroom and grab a snack and a drink so you will not have to get up in the middle of class for any reason.
- Find a seat where you can see the professor and the front of the classroom.
- You will continue through your day and repeat this process for each class.
- Lunchtime is a good time to relax, catch up with friends, and prepare for your afternoon courses.
- After classes end, take a few minutes in the library to review your notes from each class.
- Head home, take some time to relax, and then begin your homework.
- Law schools will call for you to read between ten and fifty pages per evening per class. This quickly doubles, as you generally have to read the material twice to understand exactly what it covers.
- You will carry a fifteen-hour course load, and depending upon the breakdown of daily classes, you may even average about seventy-five pages of reading on a particularly heavy homework night.
- Repeat this process every day for the next three years of your life!

Let Me Introduce You to a Few of My Friends: Your First-Year Courses

While orientation is a valuable opportunity to begin successful habits, the classes you must complete in your first year form the foundation for your journey through law school. You will be faced with an obstacle course consisting of eight challenging barriers you must overcome before moving to the next stage in the journey.

The following is a detailed list of the eight courses students must conquer in order to gain the knowledge necessary to succeed in their future endeavors. In addition, you will also find a short summary of each class, including the difficulty level of the class (hard, medium, easy), and the pros and cons of each course. Please note that all classes are extremely difficult, but some are more difficult than others (depending on the teacher, course load, and other students you are competing with in your section). Here we go . . . .

Torts

Torts focuses on the study of tort law, defined as civil wrongs found within our society. Torts fall into three categories: intentional torts (intentional acts that harm another person), negligent torts (irresponsible actions that cause injury to another), and liability torts (acts that cause injury to another without any intentional fault). Torts can be anything from assault and battery to breach of privacy issues, such as defamation. Torts include a variety of offenses, and therefore this course covers an extremely eclectic array of material.

DIFFICULTY LEVEL: Medium

POSITIVES: Interesting topics; generally straightforward, black letter law

NEGATIVES: Challenging fact patterns on exams; hard to differentiate between certain torts

---

Property

Property law focuses on the rights of individuals who own property. This property can be real property, such as land ownership, or other property, such as the right to use something. Property deals with everything from the transferring of interests in land to the rights a landowner has in relation to their land. Land ownership is the most discussed subject in these classes, and law school students are constantly faced with abstract questions as to who owns a piece of land, or any other object, in rather vague situations.

DIFFICULTY LEVEL: Hard

POSITIVES: Interesting and useful topics

NEGATIVES: Rules against perpetuities and future interests are some of the harder concepts law students will ever face

---

Contracts

Students find their way into contractual law and are often challenged with intriguing situations where contracts are broken and objects or money must be awarded. Contract law spends a great deal of time dealing with broken promises, breaches of contracts, damages, and performance outlined by a contract. Considering that the majority of Americans' work is based on contracts and working agreements, contract law carries a great significance in the educational life of a law school student.

DIFFICULTY LEVEL: Medium/Hard

POSITIVES: Extremely necessary and useful in all parts of the law; intriguing concepts, statutory rules

NEGATIVES: Interpreting statutory regulations can often be challenging and cases can be overly vague and confusing, as there is a great deal of negotiation and contractual caveats

---

Civil Procedure

Civil procedure classes concentrate on the study of issues that govern the civil courts in America. The majority of professors will teach the course using the Federal Rules of Civil Procedure as a guide. Most civil procedure classes will focus on personal jurisdiction (the courts' jurisdiction over the individual), venue (the courts' right to hear a case), pleadings, issues concerning a party's involvement and rights of participation in a lawsuit, and topics covering what a court and a party can or cannot do when bringing a claim against another person.

DIFFICULTY LEVEL: Hard

POSITIVES: Wide array of helpful supplements available for students; regulated by statute; professors work hard to simplify the tough topics

NEGATIVES: Widely considered the hardest first-year course; statutes are often vague and offer little explanation

---

Constitutional Law

Many law schools consider constitutional law a first-year course; however, I took constitutional law in my second year. Constitutional law deals with the interpretation of specific articles in the U.S. Constitution. The most important aspect of this course is the study of the decision process the Supreme Court applies when it is faced with a particular set of facts. Many professors will also discuss the commerce clause, dormant commerce clause, and other issues.

DIFFICULTY LEVEL: Hard

POSITIVES: Variety of study guides to help students; teachers generally present bare-bone concepts to students

NEGATIVES: Conceptually challenging; black letter law is constantly changing; tons of tests and flow charts

---

Criminal Law

As the name implies, criminal law focuses on law that punishes crime. Crime occurs in many shapes and forms and criminal law finds its place in the courts with regard to the right of a defendant to have a trial by jury. Other topics covered include double jeopardy, burden of proof, definitions of murder, and requisite intent.

DIFFICULTY LEVEL: Medium

POSITIVES: Statutorily based; intriguing topics; interesting case law

NEGATIVES: Necessary to be familiar with a lot of definitions; hard to differentiate between murder categories

Professional Responsibility

Few schools offer professional responsibility classes to law students in their first year. Professional responsibility classes deal with an attorney's capacity in a professional setting, including his or her duties to society, clients, and the attorney-client privilege. This class defines a lawyer's place in American society and outlines a lawyer's responsibilities and the punishments for a breach of these duties.

DIFFICULTY LEVEL: Easy

POSITIVES: Statutorily based; conceptually easy and straightforward; interesting case law; class is conducted in a discussion-focused manner

NEGATIVES: Repetitious; statutes can be vague and hard to interpret

Legal Writing

Legal writing teaches students how to draft briefs, memoranda, and other vital documents. This course requires students to gain a fundamental knowledge of the law and spotlights the art of persuasion through written legalese terminology and guidelines.

DIFFICULTY LEVEL: Hard

POSITIVES: Limited class meetings; interesting topics; no exams

NEGATIVES: Students spend a great deal of time for a reduced amount of credit; editing is challenging; involves a lot of drafts and rewrites

---

Importance of Class

After outlining the obstacles ahead, it is essential to take time to discuss how you can succeed in this new, challenging environment. The most essential element of law school is the daily classes. Therefore, the most important action you can take to find success is to attend class. In class you will be presented with the materials in a productive environment by a professor who will promote thought and provide real-world examples.

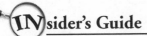 **sider's Guide**

Student Counsel

3L Peter Morris says, "Keep your notes and other class materials well organized, so you can spend more time learning and less time looking for everything you need to prepare for classes and exams."

While there are professors who allow a certain number of absences without penalty or punishment, attending class on a regular basis will certainly increase understanding and show significant gains in test scores, because professors focus much of their class time on potential exam topics. However, you must realize that attending classes is not enough. I had friends in law school that attended class and surfed the Internet, instant messaged each other, and paid attention to everything except the professor. Students must attend class *and* pay attention. Professors develop test questions based on statements they made in class. Paying attention and taking good notes during class is essential to success in law school. If you don't plan on doing this, then attending class is not very useful. You might not flunk the class for attendance reasons, but you will not succeed in the long run.

Classmates

While many new law school students are concerned with course material and first-year subjects, they often ask me what to expect from law school classmates. Law school students are an interesting breed of scholar, as they want to know everything, they think they know everything, and they really know nothing—all at the same time. Interacting with other law school students can be quite frustrating, because you are competing with one another, but you often need one another's help. Imagine two NFL teams playing each other in the Super Bowl. Both teams are trying to win the game, but their coaches traded playbooks before the game started. Imagine that mess. Law school can be similar to this. You want to compete, but you can't help answering your colleagues' and friends' questions when they have them.

I have heard stories from other first-year students about people actually tearing the pages out of research books so other students cannot find the answers to the assigned questions. The most important thing to expect and remember is that you are all in the same boat. In your first year, you are all learning the same material, experiencing the same challenges, and competing for the same prize. The most important thing you should remember in your first year is to be friendly, be helpful, and to meet as many people as you can. Law students are generally friendly people who want all the help they can get. That one student you were rude to in your first-year contracts course could one day become a district court judge and you might find yourself in her court, where she can make your life miserable. Be cordial, be polite, and help others to the best of your ability, because you never know when that outline you gave to some random kid in school will end up helping you out when you are in a bind. As cliché as it sounds, what goes around comes around. Law school is a huge circle and if you pass on the wealth, you will receive some in return.

Sections

Many law schools organize their first-year students by sections. Each section includes a specific number of students who have the same curriculum for their first year. While all first-year students will have the same course load during their first year, all the students in a specific section will have the same professors, class schedules, and classrooms. Dividing first-year students into sections has noticeable advantages and disadvantages, including some of the following:

Advantages:
- Students become friendly with a large group of their colleagues quickly.
- Students can form groups to work on their outlines and classwork.
- Students find comfort in knowing many of their classmates right from the start.
- Classes may be smaller, allowing more focused time with the professors.

Disadvantages:
- First-year students will be limited to everyday interactions with their sections and may not have many opportunities to meet other students.
- There is no flexibility in class scheduling, as the student must fit the section rather than the section fitting the student.
- Students may not be happy with their sections, and they are stuck with the same group of students for the entire year.

- Sections take away the novelty that many classes offer by providing different personalities and opinions, as often the same students speak in class.

By no means would I say schools that section their students are better or worse than other schools. This is simply an administrative decision that has potential pros and cons on each side of the spectrum. Whatever the case may be, students still need to prepare for class, study hard, and pay attention to their professors.

Preparing for Classes

While class will play an important role in your everyday law school life, class proves to be unhelpful if you are not prepared and comfortable with the material presented. Law school professors are in your face and will not hesitate to call upon you and push the limits of your mind and confidence. Through solid preparation, you can duel with the professor and even impress him with abstract thought and stimulating connections. Law school is not a game of catch-up, but rather an intricately designed process that calls for you to be responsible, prepare for class, and dedicate your mind to the learning process in the institution. Josh Epstein, a second-year law school student at the University of Texas School of Law states, "The people I know that have done well have treated it like a job. Unlike undergrad school, you have to do all the reading as it's assigned—if not then you won't have a clue what's going on in class, and it is too much to cram in at the end." Mr. Epstein's comments present the essential point that law school calls for preparation and consistency. Being prepared for class by doing the readings is a great step to take to become a successful law school graduate.

Classroom Routine

As a first-year law student, you should be particularly familiar with the daily classroom routine. If you are not, you will learn pretty quickly. During the first year of law school, the "all-knowing" professor runs classes using the Socratic method. The Socratic method is based on a few underlying principles that foster unique and original thinking from students.

To begin with, the Socratic method calls for the professor to ask questions and for the students to provide the answers to those questions. While the students may also ask questions about the subject matter, many times the professor will reverse the situation and put the ball back in the students' court.

The second rule of the Socratic method is that it is the professor's class and the professor's course material. Therefore, the law school classroom is somewhat of a battlefield where the professor plays the role of Goliath and the students play the role of David. However, the difference in this story is that David does not always win. The professor usually wins every situation because he has all the answers. It adds an even better twist when the professor wrote the book you are assigned. This is common in law school and all but kills the "bullshit factor." The BS factor is a skill students use in hopes of persuading professors that they know the answer when they are really just full of it. The BS factor does not work in law school. Many students made a living off of the BS factor in undergraduate school, but in law school you have to remember that many of your professors wrote your course books and can cut through your BS quicker than you can spell it. If you don't know the answer, be honest and the professor might let you get away with a slap on the hand, and a "please be better prepared next time" lecture.

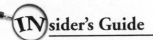 **IN)sider's Guide**

Professor Pointer

Professor Doug Isenberg says, "If you take notes by hand, consider typing them after class to reinforce what you've learned and to further your organization; if you take notes on a computer, print them out regularly (and/or back them on another disk) to avoid the devastation a 'system crash' could cause."

In short, the professor knows the information and the students are learning the information. Many times students become disoriented and upset with the daily routine because it often seems like a no-win situation. Thus, it is important to accept from the start that you are receiving an education and all the obstacles and annoyances you are going through are growing pains and part of the education process. Remember, law school is a learning process and the professor is not there to hurt your future aspirations to become a lawyer. Law school professors play a devil's advocate role that forces students to think and rethink statements and situations and gain the ability to support any argument or stance that they may take.

Reviewing after Class

When you leave the classroom and depart from the professors, the most important part of the learning process begins. You are equipped with a large number of resources and skills to work through the obstacles that law school courses present. To begin with, a useful skill is reviewing notes and information directly after class. Taking fifteen minutes after class to review previous notes and fill in any questions or gaps will increase your proficiency, comprehension, and retention, because the information will be fresh in your mind. Law school courses are often demanding and the amount of information covered in a short period of time is intimidating. However, reviewing notes directly after class will improve your notes and eliminate any confusion months later.

Professors

Another useful technique you can apply to increase your chances of success is to use professors as resources outside of class. After class, professors will meet with you to discuss topics and issues covered in class. Because students rarely understand everything covered in class, professors are more than willing to answer questions when class is over, in a more comfortable and intimate setting. In addition to meeting with professors directly after class, all professors offer office hours in which you can discuss issues in a one-on-one session. Professors will rarely offer answers without discussion or thought, but they are often more than willing to answer individual concerns when you display extra effort and meet with them in their offices outside of class. If nothing else, it is worth meeting with a professor to ask questions without the barriers the Socratic method creates in the classroom. This will enable you to ask questions and actually receive straightforward answers. It really makes things a lot easier than the Socratic method approach, where questions are often answered with more questions. A professor will be more likely to show you her cards when you meet with her outside of class.

Studying

Aside from attending classes, studying is the most vital part of a law school student's life. Brian Abramson, a student at the University of Texas Law School, says, "I have always been a pretty hard worker, but the difference is how you have to study. There is no point in reading if you don't understand the material. It often takes me longer to get through the reading because I am not just trying to get through it as quickly as possible. Outlining is also something I never did in undergrad, but you can take outlines into the final, so this is to your advantage." Studying is indeed a central part of law school and there is a strong correlation between longer, more focused studying hours and higher test scores.

In addition to the importance of studying, we must also discuss the most efficient ways to actually get the studying done. Many law school students fight an internal battle as to where to focus their efforts. Will professors ask exam questions centered on details? Or will professors ask for an understanding of the big picture and show little interest in the ability to memorize paltry details? Unfortunately, the answer lies somewhere in between. Law school requires you to understand the entire picture and have the innate ability to make unseen connections and pull together seemingly unrelated pieces to form a harmonious combination. This is imperative to succeeding in law school. Taking separate sections of the law and piecing them together is a skill every lawyer must have. It is crucial to consider and fully grasp all of the particulars in order to comprehend the whole. Otherwise, students will never truly understand and be able to resourcefully use the law.

Summary

Law school and the challenges it presents could quite possibly be described as the most intriguing and mind-altering experience you will ever have. The curriculum will push you to your limit. This is done for a reason, and I guarantee you will not leave law school as the same person you were when you entered. Success comes only with great sacrifice and dedication to the curriculum and the work. You must study the basic obstacles law school presents, focus on adequate preparation, polish your writing skills, take the outlined guidelines to heart, and put forth a conscious effort to implement these skills in your daily work. Once you can do this, law school will inevitably create a more rewarding learning environment, leading to a greater understanding of the material and a blossoming of your mind.

CHAPTER TWO

Preparing for the Cl-ass Kicking of Your Life

AUGUST 25, 2003

This Sure Isn't College

Off to a great start. I survived my contracts course with just a minor embarrassment: the first, but certainly not the last. I have three more wonderful years of swallowing my pride and learning from my mistakes. The bright shade of red once covering my face is now a milder, more ghostly complexion. After contracts I made my way to the library to prepare for my next class. I had forty-five minutes to get my act together. I pulled out my book, I snagged a syllabus off the Internet, I found the rainbow of highlighters in the bottom of my backpack, and I turned on my laptop. I began reading, rereading, highlighting, rehighlighting, and rethinking what I am doing in law school. Focus. I hit the books, finish the reading, and briskly walk into class as the professor is taking his final glance over the nervous and inept classroom. Game time. The teacher begins speaking, and I am already lost. Civil procedure, why do you sound Greek to me? I stress, I get hot flashes, I pray the teacher does not look at me. I hear my least favorite words in the English language: "Mr. Spizman, please define civil procedure." I must be the most unlucky kid in the world. Two classes, two call outs. I think quickly and blurt out, "It is the study of the steps and procedures civil litigants may take as their case proceeds through the courtroom."

Bullshit. Wrong. What am I thinking? The professor gives me a good once over, turns to another student, and says, "Mr. Hart, can you define civil procedure?" 0-1. At least he isn't asking me any more questions.

What's the Big Deal about Class?

Good question. Now remember, we aren't talking about the way you carry yourself through life or the social barriers between the rich and the poor; that is another book for another time. The type of class I am talking about is professor v. students, students v. casebook, students v. distractions, and students v. preparation. The type of class I am talking about is the constant struggle between the right answer and the wrong answer. Class may be overwhelming, but this chapter will provide you with a bounty of helpful hints and tools you can implement into your nightly reading and your daily class routine. Class is your opportunity to exhibit your knowledge and understanding of the course material. It is a time to ask questions and clarify any gaps or confusion that may have arisen from your reading. Class is an extremely valuable resource, and the work and preparation you put into class may be the difference between an A and a C.

This chapter will focus on classroom attendance, classroom preparation, the briefing process, and classroom etiquette. Remember that law school is a far cry from college. Many times in college the bare minimum will lead to success. However, law school is significantly different, especially in the first year. It is impossible to succeed in law school using the same classroom and study habits you may have used in college. This is a new and unique situation, and you must be liquid and adapt to your new surroundings.

Attendance

As cliché as it sounds, "You practice how you play." End of story, enough said. The most successful law students are the ones who attend class. If you do not attend class in an effective and prepared manner, you are selling your educational experience short, and you simply will not have the ability to succeed. Surprisingly enough, many of the concepts and statements professors cover during class appear front and center on exam day (note the sarcasm).

I am a realist. I understand there will be times when you simply cannot attend class. Sickness, religious holidays, interviews, important meetings, work for other classes, and plain old laziness may all be "viable" excuses, but it is important to miss only the bare minimum of your classes. You are not paying thousands of dollars just to attend law school and take exams; you pay tuition each semester to receive an education and to be part of an intricate and complicated learning process. If you do not attend class, you will not be part of this learning process. It is a waste of time and money.

The attendance process is pretty simple stuff. The teacher usually has a role sheet and passes it throughout the classroom. It is your responsibility to sign your name on it as there is always a chance the attendance sheet may miss you. That being said, make sure you put forth the effort to find the sheet and sign it before you leave class. The last thing you want to do is attend class and not get credit for it. If for some reason you forgot to sign the attendance sheet, be sure to e-mail the professor and let her know. Always stay on top of your attendance and always remember to sign in.

On the first day of class, read the syllabus and note the attendance requirements. Most professors will allow you to miss only a certain number of classes before you are unable to sit for the final exam. Note how many unexcused absences you have in each course and be sure to track your absences anytime you miss a class. Always remember that absences can make or break your grade. Many times you can meet with professors and review your exams to see exactly where you went wrong. If your exam grade is only one point short of a grade break (e.g., receiving an 89 when a 90 is an A), the professor may be more inclined to give you the extra point if you can exhibit your understanding of the material and have perfect attendance in class. Classroom participation demonstrates your dedication. So that one sick day could potentially be the difference between an A and a B.

However, attending class is only part of the battle. It is essential to be prepared and familiar with the assigned material for that class. Coming to class unprepared is as useful as not coming to class at all. While the professor is presenting complicated concepts and theories, you will have no understanding of the principles behind these ideas. Take a look at my first day of class in civil procedure. My situation could have easily been avoided with proper preparation and knowledge of basic concepts such as the definition of the course topic. While the teacher may make you look like a fool on many occasions, it should never be a direct result of being under-prepared. Remember, all the answers are right in front of you in your casebook; it is just a matter of knowing them when class begins.

The "Foolish Scenario"

So how can you avoid experiencing the embarrassment I experienced on my first day of class? Preparation is by the far the easiest and least stressful step you can take to avoid the "foolish scenario." The "foolish scenario" is the point in the class when you are called on and have no clue what the answer is. You panic and blurt out an incoherent string of legal jargon that, when put together, means absolutely nothing, thus making you look like a fool.

How Do I Avoid This?

Avoiding the "foolish scenario" starts the night before your class. The following steps will allow you to prepare for your courses in an efficient and complete manner.

Step One: On the first day of class you will receive the course syllabus. View this document as a map for the next four months of your life. Take your course syllabus and read through it multiple times, highlighting each assignment and attendance policies.

Step Two: Grab a calendar (which you should always have with you). Many students like to use programs like Microsoft Outlookto plan their course work.

Step Three: Using different highlighters for each course, mark down the assignments on your calendar. This will give you a visual aid as to the amount of work you have to complete each night.

Step Four: At the end of the day, sit down with your calendar, your books, and your laptop and begin your night's assignments.

Nightly Reading

Once you are prepared and comfortable with your assignments for each class, it is time to begin the reading. Your nightly reading will be one of—if not the most important—pieces to finding success as a 1L. Poor study habits will lead to poor performance. Take the following steps to ensure success and comprehension with each of your law school class assignments:

Alleviate distractions. Once you have received your assignment, sit down in a quiet place where you can concentrate on the material in front of you. Alleviate as many distractions as possible, as the material is challenging enough without further distractions such as the Internet, television, radio, friends, cell phones, etc.

Be prepared to study. Make sure you have the appropriate tools: study aids, highlighters, laptop, pens, drinks, snacks, etc. Once you begin focusing on the assignment, you want to maintain this focus. Repeatedly stepping away from your assignment for a drink of water or a pen will only extend your study time and inhibit your ability to fully comprehend the material. Once you begin to focus, it is helpful to maintain your concentration.

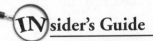

INsider's Guide

Professor Pointer

Professor Doug Isenberg says, "Always read every class assignment before every class. Outline every case you read before class begins so you are prepared for class discussion, which will allow you to get the most benefit from the classes themselves, and to boost your performance for classes where 'participation' counts."

Avoid logging on. Even if you are in the library with no distractions, connecting to the Internet to instant message or surf the Web can become extremely distracting. One minute of Web surfing can quickly turn into fifteen minutes of Internet shopping. Leave the Ethernet cord at home and focus on your studying.

Brief cases as you go. Briefing (which will be discussed in detail in the next section) is the most effective and efficient method of summarizing the cases you read. After you read through a case, take a few minutes and review your notations. Turn to study guides or case summaries to review the case law and make sure you are on the right track. At this point you should have a solid understanding of the case and have the ability to create a useful and effective case brief.

Review your notes. Congratulations on finishing your assignments for the next full day of classes. However, you are not done just yet. Always arrive for class a few minutes early so you can review the assignment and reread each of your case briefs. All of your hard work will be useless if you cannot even remember the case law.

Case Briefing

Widely considered the most important part of law school, case briefing is the process of summarizing each case in a clear and concise manner. The following is a step-by-step guide to briefing a case. Each element of the case-briefing process has its own purpose and value that will help you understand the assigned case.

What Are the Essential Pieces of the Case-Briefing Process?

Cause of action. This defines the clear and concise reason the claim is before the court. This generally identifies both the plaintiff(s) and defendant(s) in the court case, as well as the plaintiff's claim against the defendant. It can also be helpful to specify which court the case is in (i.e., federal v. state) and what type of case this is (i.e., civil v. criminal).

Procedural posture. Consider the procedural posture a map of the case's history. Many cases begin at one point and end at a different point in a different court. Within this element of the case-briefing process, students look at each piece of the case from the initial claims to appeals, decisions, reversals, remands, and final decisions. It is vital to understanding the present case to see exactly how the case moved through the court system and how it arrived at its present point. Plot each movement the case has made along with the court's decisions along the way. Higher courts place a great deal of value and emphasis on lower courts' judgments, and it is important to see exactly why they agree or disagree with previous decisions.

Facts. Each case has its own unique set of facts. In a detailed fashion, organize the essential points of the case, identifying how the disagreement came to a head. The best way to do this is in timeline form, because it gives you a better understanding of the events that lead to the adjudication. Separate each independent fact into a single bullet point so you will be better prepared to answer questions the professor may ask.

Issues. This is the most important part of your briefing process. The issue is a single, concise statement identifying the reason the parties are in court. A good issue statement will isolate the legal issue involved in the case. It may be helpful to phrase the issue in question form so you will have a clear yes-or-no answer to the statement, which will guide you in the court's general decision and thought process.

Ruling. The ruling is generally the answer to your issue question. This element of the case-briefing process asks you to find out exactly who the court agreed with. It is also valuable to note whether the court reversed or remanded a lower court's decision while making its own.

Court reasoning. The court's reasoning is the process by which the court arrived at the final decision. Use this section to summarize the case law and important precedent that the court used in arriving at their ruling. Within this section it may be helpful to create two separate columns to itemize both the plaintiff's and the defendant's arguments. This will allow you the opportunity to see exactly which arguments the court found effective and which it did not care for.

Analysis. This final section is an opportunity to reflect on the court's decision and analyze the thought process behind the decision, as well as the future precedent this case may set. Ask questions like: Will this decision change current law? How will this affect cases with similar facts? Does this overturn previous decisions?

Answers to these questions will not only help you understand the courts reasoning, but will also give you a simplified and in-depth legal perspective to tough case law.

Dog Days

There are going to be days when you simply cannot read for class. You will not be prepared, you will not have any idea what is going on, and you will not have the answers to the professor's questions . . . or will you? Here is a list of steps you can take to avoid those dog days and have all the answers, even when reading and preparation are just not possible.

Case briefs. Study guides and commercial outlines will be discussed in detail later on, but these can be useful tools if you simply do not have the time to prepare for class. Never use them as a replacement for your nightly reading. Even after class has ended, go back and read the assignment when you have extra time. Running through your case briefs and commercial outlines will provide you with a bare-bones comprehension of the case so you will at least know the facts and issues if the professor happens to call on you.

LexisNexis and Westlaw. Both of these legal search engines provide users with case briefs detailing the facts and decision of each case in your casebook. If you are not prepared, it may be helpful to pull up these useful resources on your laptop and quickly read through the case briefs.

Friends. Another valuable resource comes from your classmates. Get to class early and ask your friends what the cases were about. If they have done the reading, they will be able to give you a basic understanding of the case law and a quick overview as to the assignment.

Breeze through the case. Lucky for you, many casebooks actually lay out the case with basic headers that will allow you to quickly scan the case to get a basic understanding of the material. Glance through the first few paragraphs of the case and the last few paragraphs, as this should provide you with the facts, the issue, and the decision, which may be enough to get you through the first few questions.

Each of these tools should be a "break only in case of emergency" resource. It is important to prepare for class each and every night and only use these tips when you simply cannot read. I neither suggest nor support using these habitually—only use them in emergency situations, and even then, go back and prepare the assignment whenever you catch up with the rest of your life.

Class Is in Session

Once you have prepared for class and have reviewed the assignment, you are now ready to focus on your "in-class skills." As mentioned above, class attendance weighs heavily on your ability to succeed as a 1L. However, attending class is just the beginning. Once there, you must pay attention and take notes in a meaningful and effective manner. Here is a list of effective tools and helpful hints you can incorporate into your classroom routine to increase success in your first year.

Note: I am a University of Texas at Austin graduate and a diehard football fan. The slogan for Texas football fans is "Come early, be loud, stay late." You might never have thought football and law school go hand in hand, but this statement has particular value for classroom success.

Come Early (to Class)

Review. Get to each one of your classes ten minutes early and reread your case briefs and notes. This will familiarize you with the material for the day, and if you are called on, you will be ready to provide a quick and correct answer.

Talk to your classmates. If you have any questions about the previous night's reading, this is a great time to sit down and receive a few other perspectives on any given case. This will also allow you the opportunity to crosscheck your understanding of the case with others, as your classmate may have caught something that you missed.

Avoid tardiness. Getting to class early allows you to find your seat, get settled, and turn on your laptop so you will be ready to roll when the professor begins speaking. I have heard stories of professors counting students absent or even disallowing them to sit down in class if they show up after class has begun. Have respect for the professor and your fellow students by making sure you are seated when class actually begins.

Be Loud (in Class)

Ask questions. Class is an opportunity to receive direct answers to complicated questions. Generally speaking, you will not be the only student confused by a statement or a concept. Courses in law school build on one another. Thus, if you miss just one concept, you may be lacking the foundation for the rest of the course. Do not be shy. Raise your hand if you ever get lost or confused during class.

Make comments. In addition to asking questions, making comments not only illustrates that you are prepared, but also shows the professor that you are an intelligent and active student. Professors will be more inclined to go out of their way to help you when they know you are sincerely interested and prepared for class. Remember, however, that it will not helpful to anyone if your comments are not well thought out. Try to participate, but do not talk just to talk, as professors will be less inclined to call on you if they know you will not provide in-depth and intelligent analysis.

Volunteer. Many times professors will call on students for the answers. However, there will be situations when the professor will throw out questions to the entire class. This is a great opportunity to participate in class and volunteer to answer questions. Professors love student volunteers, and they will be less likely to call on you if they know you will participate when you have something to say.

Stay Late (in Class)

Review. Go back to the ten-minute rule once class ends. Take ten minutes and sit in front of your notes from that day and review them. This will allow you to fill in any gaps in your notes, which is important because weeks later there is no chance you will know what you meant to write down. This is also a great skill to aid in retention. Multiple studies have shown that just ten minutes of review after class can help you retain and understand the material better, alleviating the strain when it is exam time.

Talk to your professors. Make sure you have a good communication network with all of your professors. It is very easy to meet and greet professors directly after class, because they will usually be speaking to students and answering any questions they may still have. Take this opportunity to schedule meetings, ask other questions, or chat about anything you can think of. It is always advantageous for your professors to know who you are, which will only happen through your efforts.

Remember the University of Texas football slogan, "Come early, be loud, stay late." Following these three simple steps will help ensure your success as a 1L. Just as football players review game films every week before a game, you should also focus your efforts to be prepared when it is game time. And do not be deterred if you ask a silly question or do not know the answer to a question the professor asks. Just as when the star quarterback throws an interception, there will always be another opportunity to make up for your mistake. Learn the lesson and be better prepared to throw a touchdown the next time around.

Study Guides

What are study guides? Study guides are commercial resources created by professors and legal scholars. They provide readers with an explanation of cases, theories, and concepts. Many times, they go hand in hand with specific casebooks as helpful resources to understand the often wordy and confusing material. Study guides come in a number of forms.

Commercial Outlines

Commercial outlines are generally long and in-depth outlines of an entire course. They present all of the theories that the specific course will cover and pose many different hypotheticals and fact patterns, which allow students the ability to deal with different issues. They are helpful to fill in gaps in your notes and outlines, but are simply too large to use as anything more than a supplement to the outlines you have created.

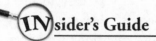

Insider's Guide

Professor Pointer

Professor Roy Sobelson says, "Students might want to rethink how they approach classes. I think students should brief cases all through law school, arriving in class with a good brief and maybe even questions of their own about the cases. In class, they should probably spend more time listening to and participating in class discussions than writing things down. Taking time to reread cases afterward will allow the students to refine their briefs and understanding of the cases, as well as go over the class discussion one more time. You'd be surprised how your understanding of difficult class material may improve when you think it over outside the pressure-filled classroom environment."

Case Briefs

Case briefs are study guides that simply brief each case in your casebook. They provide students with each element of the case-briefing process. These are great to use to refresh your memory and crosscheck your case briefs against those of the professionals.

Examples and Explanations

Examples and explanations are wonderful study guides. They present each course concept in a direct manner. Each chapter is well organized and walks students through each piece of the concept, tying it all together at the end of each chapter. E and Es also present a ton of hypothetical questions throughout the chapter along with detailed answers to each. These are extremely useful, because they provide exam-type questions and tricky fact patterns that may appear on the exam.

Students and professors alike are split on the issue of study guides. It is important to walk a thin line when using commercial outlines and case briefs. In my opinion, these resources can be helpful study aids if used correctly. However, by no means should study guides act as replacements for your classroom reading. In fact, overusing these resources can be particularly detrimental, because you will only have a bare-bones understanding of the material, which is all they usually offer. So the question remains, exactly where do we draw the line?

Helpful Ways to Use Outlines and Briefs

Read first. It is extremely important to sit down and read the casebook before you dive into the case briefs. You may miss some concepts in the casebook, but you will have a better understanding of the material if you read it in its entirety. Most case briefs give readers an overview of the case with little in-depth analysis. Thus, reading the entire case before the summaries will allow you a fuller understanding of the material.

Crosscheck your briefs. After reading the cases on your own, case briefs and study guides may be very effective tools. Study guides fill in gaps in the case and provide readers with a better understanding of the case decision, which can save you time and effort when you review the cases. Taking a few minutes to cross-reference your briefs against those in the commercial outlines after you read may provide you with a greater understanding of the material and ensure that you pulled the main points from each case.

Don't overuse study guides. Be careful with the number of study guides you use and the value you place on them. It may be especially helpful to use study guides during exam time to review general concepts and overall theories; however, it is important to focus on the case law during the semester. Read the cases with the subtle aid of study guides. Use them as a guiding hand rather than a controlling force.

Review case briefs before class. Using commercial case briefs before class is generally pretty helpful. Take a few minutes before each class period and sit down with your briefs and the case outlines. This will refresh your memory and prepare you to participate.

Don't cite commercial cases. Many commercial outlines and case briefs discuss cases that may fall under the theory you are discussing but are not presented in your casebook. Be careful to focus only on those cases the professor presents directly from the casebook. To begin with, the professor will be testing you on the authority in the casebook, not in your commercial outlines. While thinking outside the box is wonderful, it is important to focus on the case law in your course book, as it may be in direct conflict with, or different from, other case law. Secondly, law school professors are wise beyond their years, and if you pull a case out of left field, they will know you are relying on a commercial outline. So long as you are prepared by creating your own case briefs and outline, quoting another authority may be impressive and show the professor you have put in your due diligence.

Study guides can truly be helpful and increase success in your first year of law school so long as you use them in an effective manner and never rely on them as a replacement for nightly reading. If you purchase these books from consumer Web sites such as Amazon or eBay you will be able to purchase lightly used books for less than half the price as in the stores.

Classroom Etiquette

Just as important as attending class, preparing for class, and participating in class is how you carry yourself during the actual class. Good manners and etiquette will allow you to better network with your classmates and your professors. Here is a list of classroom "do's" and "don'ts."

Do

Be polite. The most important lesson you should incorporate into your classroom routine is "always be polite." There will be times when you disagree with the professor, your classmates, and even the casebook. However, there is a right way and a wrong way to voice your thoughts. Do not be impolite and eccentric with your remarks. Present your opinion in a respectful manner, because the last thing you want to do is disrespect or upset your classmates or your professor.

Turn off your phone. Question: What is the quickest way to annoy your professor? Answer: Choose "When the Saints Go Marching In" as your cell phone ringer and have your mom call you during class. Seriously, though, professors hate it with an undying, everlasting passion when cell phones go off in class. They not only interrupt the learning process, but also the professor's thought process, and anything and everything else productive within the classroom. I always like to be on the safe side, so as I am walking into the classroom, I turn off my cell phone and leave it in my backpack; that way, no temptation arises to text a friend or mess with it during class.

Be assertive. When you speak in class, be assertive. Be confident in your statements and support them with strong case law and valid arguments. The other students and your professor will have more respect for you if you participate in an assertive and well thought out manner. It is okay to make a mistake. Everyone slips at one point in law school. The important thing is to at least try.

Be prepared. Would you go to a meeting with a client unprepared? Would you sit at a dinner table and eat with your hands? Both of these are extremely impolite and similar to entering a law school class unprepared: It is impolite and improper etiquette. Professors expect students to understand the reading and, at the bare minimum, know the facts and the outcome of the cases.

Don't

Be argumentative. Treat law school classes like you treat your friends and family: with respect. Do not be argumentative with your classmates and your professors. Respect each and every one of them and you will receive the same in return. Classroom discussions touch on many sensitive issues and students will approach these issues with passion and emotion. Remember to present your arguments in a respectful manner and be consistently aware of the situation and your classmates' feelings.

Leave your computer volume on. Just like your cell phone, make sure you turn off the volume on your computer. There is nothing worse than sitting in class, falling into the temptation of checking *www.ESPN.com* just for a second, and then having everyone in the room hear Stuart Scott give his 30 at 30 news update because you forgot to turn off the volume on your computer.

Chat with your neighbors. Do I seriously need to flesh this one out? Pay attention in class and do not be disrespectful by talking with your neighbors. If a question arises, I generally do one of two things: I write a quick note to the person sitting next to me to ask a question, or I write down my question on a piece of paper and at a break in the classroom action, I raise my hand and ask the professor about it. There is no need to talk directly to your neighbors, and professors will have no patience for the excessive noise and bothersome comments.

Be tardy. Always get to class early. There is no excuse for being late, and if you know you will be tardy, send your professor an e-mail letting him know why and when you will be there. Walking into class late interrupts the learning process and greatly annoys professors.

Leave early. Similar to arriving late is leaving early. Avoid leaving class before it ends at all costs. If you know you have a conflict and will need to leave early, communicate with the professor before class begins and let her know when you will be leaving and for what reason. Furthermore, make sure you sit in a place that is easily accessible to the aisle and the exit so you do not bother your classmates when you leave.

BS your professors. Never, ever, in a thousand years, try to BS your way through an answer. It is improper etiquette and ridiculously annoying. The professors know all of the answers. Seriously. A few of them will have written your course books. Your BS has no chance in law school classrooms. If you do not know the answer, simply say that and the professor will move on.

Class Over

This chapter should have you prepared for law school's rigorous classroom experience. Success begins with preparing for class, attending class, and actively participating in class. This will allow you a better opportunity to receive clarity when you are confused. Class is what your tuition is for and you are cheating yourself by not taking full advantage of all the wonderful resources the classroom setting has to offer. Remember the Texas Longhorns' slogan: "Come early, be loud, stay late."

OCTOBER 17, 2003

Crash

5:50 P.M. Class starts in ten minutes. Damn Atlanta traffic. I am sitting in my car, giving a ride to a friend, bumper-to-bumper traffic, and I'm one mile away from the Georgia State exit. . . . So close, yet so far. Urban sprawl is ruining my life. I slam on the gas—let's roll. Brakes. Gas. Brakes. One hundred yards away, light at the end of the tunnel. I see an opening in the left-hand lane, so I gun it. The car behind me cuts me off; I swerve back into my lane and the car in front of me stops short. Crash. I rear-end the lady in front of me. She is pissed. My car has had better days. We pull over and wait for the cops to arrive. I am in law school, so I know my ticket for "following too closely" is right around the corner. My classmate is not happy. She turns to me and firmly states, "Well, smart move grabbing a ride with you." I am not happy. Finally the cops arrive. I approach the cop car, apologize for the incident and explain that my friend and I are late for class. The other officer offers to give my friend a ride to class. She steps in the back of the cop car, behind two inches of bullet-proof glass and gating. They drive off—lights flashing and everything. The full effect: hilarious. Probably even worth the damage that has just occurred. As my car is being hooked up to the tow truck and the kind officer is writing my ticket, I call a classmate and ask to speak to the professor. I apologize for being late, explain the situation, and thank him for understanding. He pauses for a moment and says, "Mr. Spizman, you have totaled your car, you are getting a ticket, and you are in the middle of the highway. With all of these circumstances, you still thought to call me to tell me you will be late? Thank you. I am flattered, but I feel like you have a few more pressing issues on your plate right now than being a few minutes tardy for my class. Good luck. Drive more carefully next time."

Picking Your Profs

While the above story was not one of my proudest law school moments, it could have been worse. This event happened midway through the first semester, and I had previously attended office hours, scheduled meetings, and casually spoken to my professor on a regular basis. Not only did I not receive an absence for my wreck, but the professor also e-mailed me his class notes to ensure I was prepared for his exam. Little did I know the following summer I would not only be working for this professor, but also writing an independent study under his guidance. The point remains, and this story illustrates, that using your professors as resources can prove to be one of the most useful and powerful tools you have at your disposal.

Picking your professors is one of the easiest ways to meaningfully impact your first year of law school. Your professors may be the difference between a pleasant semester and a strikingly difficult one. Think about it. Just a few minutes of research and effort before you choose your professors will make all the difference in the next six months of your life. Sounds like a good deal to me.

Many law schools across the country provide students with their first-year curriculums. Furthermore, many of these law schools also place students into specific sections. Each section has a set schedule along with specific professors assigned to students by the school itself. However, if you are one of the fortunate students attending a law school that allows you to pick your professors for your first-year curriculum, take full advantage of this leniency and make your choices count.

Attorney Advice

Attorney Jessica Gordon says, "In your first year, you should start asking 2Ls and 3Ls about their favorite professors. My advice: Try to choose as many classes as you can based on recommendations of which professors to take from students who have gone before you. To make relationships early on with older students, join at least one or two clubs within your first semester. This will help you to get to know your classmates in a different setting. Often, clubs will have lists of favorite professors. These professors will make even the most daunting or seemingly dry subject interesting and exciting, while other professors may take an exciting subject and make it dry. Caveat: If you want to go into a particular legal field, such as employment law, and the only professor teaching that class is not recommended, you should still take the class. Sometimes you need to choose based on subject. For all other times, however, choose based on professor."

Avoiding the Tough Guys

So you are allowed to pick your first-year professors, but how do you effectively choose the right professors when you are an entering student with little knowledge of your new law school or the professors? There are some simple resources you can use to help choose the best professor for you.

Talk to Older Students

Always remember to use your resources. Older students have been there and have done what you are about to do. During your orientation program, there will be a great deal of second- and third-year students on campus mentoring incoming 1Ls, all ready and able to answer any questions you may have about your new professors. These students volunteered to be part of the orientation program and will be friendly and extremely open to answering any questions you may have.

Use Your Mentors

Many law schools involve first-year students in a mentor program, assigning an older student to each new student. This is an extremely valuable and easily accessible resource to use when selecting your courses. Stay in contact with your mentor, and when it is time to register for classes during your first year, ask specific questions and find out what professors your mentor had and his or her feelings about those professors.

Use Your Law School Web Page

Most law schools have Web sites you that can view from the comfort of your home (or the library, which may become your second home during your first year). Generally speaking, there will be a professor list on this Web site with short bios of each professor. These bios are great resources. Age especially can tell a great deal about professor, although it should never be a defining factor when you choose your courses. Older professors may be more conservative and teach courses in their own manner because they may be tenured and have more job security, whereas younger professors may be more "by the book" and conscious about your first-year experience since they were there not too long ago. It is vital to your success to use every resource you have at your fingertips, even if they rely on generalizations and logical inferences, as you will be relying on logical inferences for the next three years of your life.

Use Internet Resources

There are a few Web sites out there that, for a nominal fee, will give you all of the information about your potential professors you will ever need. From general grade distributions to student reviews and ratings, these Web sites allow students to gain a snapshot of each professor and the courses they teach. These Web sites also classify professors according to each specific class they teach, allowing students a realistic representation of the specific course for which they are registering. Such Web sites include *www.PickA Prof.com*, *www.RateMyProfessors.com*, and *www.StudentReviews. com*. Some of these Web sites call for registration fees before using their services, but they are relatively affordable and provide invaluable information to incoming students.

Meet the Professors

During orientation, you will have the opportunity to meet many of your future professors. Furthermore, you will have the opportunity to talk to them in a relaxed and informal setting before classes begin. A face-to-face meeting will give you an opportunity to create your own impressions of them and even ask them specific questions about their courses and teaching styles. Trust your instincts and if you feel particularly comfortable with a certain professor, do not hesitate to register for her courses.

View Old Syllabi and Exams

Another useful step you can take when choosing your professors is to review their prior course syllabi and exams. Many professors have attendance policies, course descriptions, and course requirements on previous syllabi. Many of these syllabi and exams are easily accessible on your law school Web page. Take a few minutes and download the course syllabi to see how your expectations fit with a professor's requirements. For example, if you consider yourself to be a poor writer, then minimizing the writing requirements in your course load may be in your best interest. Some professors offer students a lenient attendance policy, while others may break down the grading into multiple tests instead of one final. You know yourself the best. Choose your professors realistically and play to your strengths.

The Initial Introduction

Once you have organized your courses and registered, the real fun begins. It is now time to actually attend class and meet your professors (if you have not already done so). Cliché alert: You only have one shot to make a good first impression. This is just like any other introduction you have ever made in your professional or personal life. Your number one responsibility is to make a positive and lasting impression.

Law school professors may seem intimidating and unapproachable at first, but the fact of the matter is that they are educators and are responsible for your well-being and career. In spite of how they may act during class, law school professors are part of your team and are rooting for your success. That being said, lesson number one concerning your initial introduction to your professor is to be confident and courteous. If you have made it to your first law school class, you are already a success. There is no need to feel intimidated. Furthermore, when you approach your professors for the initial introduction, be courteous and humble. While your professors are in your corner, it still is extremely important to show them respect, particularly when you first meet them.

Hints for Professor Introductions

Address them properly. With the initial introduction, refer to the professor as "Professor _____" (inserting their last name).

Use your full name. Always introduce yourself with a firm handshake and use your full name. Most professors will have a facebook with your full name at their disposal. However, it is extremely useful to make a formal introduction, because it will leave your new professor with a memorable first impression.

Give them something to remember. As silly as it seems, you need to differentiate yourself from other students when you introduce yourself to your professors. An easy way to accomplish this is to tell them where you are from, what college you attended, and even what you are most looking forward to learning in their course. This will put a few distinct characteristics in their mind when they think about you as a student and personalize things so you are never just another number.

Repetition. Speak to your professors on a regular basis. While you are sitting in class, think of one good question you can ask your professor after class. This will illustrate your interest in and knowledge of the course material and give you yet another excuse to speak directly with your professors in a less formal setting.

Keep it casual. Professors are human and have plenty of interests outside of law. Many times, they will be sports fans, movie snobs, music gurus, and everything in between. I once had a professor who had an undying hatred for an unnamed movie rental store and their suspect late fees. He must have begun every class with yet another story about his late charges. Plenty of students would approach him after class and discuss their mutual dislike of said movie rental company. The point is that even the smallest of topics may give you a passing hint as to a potential conversation starter with your professors. Talk to them about your interests and create a casual and personal relationship along with your professional and student relationship. This will only help you in the long run when you need a professor's help or recommendation for a clerkship or other job opportunity, because they will be able to speak about your character as well as your scholastic abilities.

Know something about them. With a little research, you can prepare yourself and demonstrate that you are knowledgeable about your professors. The best starting point is your professor bios on the law school Web site, which provide valuable information such as awards and designations they have won, current and previous law firms they have worked for, and their specialties and educational training. This will provide you with discussion topics. Who knows—maybe you two are alumni from the same college.

Never undervalue the power of a good first impression. Becoming friendly with your professors and networking with them has many advantages. Not only will it help you in school, but it is useful when you are applying for clerkships and jobs as well.

Don't Be Scared, Be Prepared

Professors can be particularly intimidating, especially in the first semester and during the first few class meetings. Remember my first experience in contracts class when I was embarrassed in front of my entire section? However, there is no need for you to be concerned or scared if you are properly prepared. Referring to the class preparation chapter will provide you with all of the necessary steps to be prepared for whatever questions and problems your professor presents during each meeting.

⌕ INsider's Guide

Attorney Advice

Attorney Jessica Gordon says, "This is one of the key predictors of success in law school and in your legal career. Get to know your professors early on. Go to office hours early in the semester. Do not just show up and claim general confusion. You should have the reading done and be prepared with one or two concrete, well thought out, substantive questions. You want your first impression to be a good one. After you establish that you are engaged in the class subject, you can talk to the professor about his or her career path and your desired path. Ask advice and forge the relationship. This can help with getting a research position during law school with that professor, getting recommendations later on, getting help with your law review note, and possible tips on where to find future employment. While you may find success in using the services provided by the career office at your school, you will likely find that the best help you can get is from faculty members with whom you have forged solid relationships."

In addition to your daily reading and outlining, there are a few tricks and tips that you can implement in your preparation to "outsmart" your professors and make a preemptive strike. Keep in mind that you must always be respectful in the classroom setting and you will never truly "outsmart" your professors, but there are numerous helpful hints which will allow you to prepare answers to questions that professors are likely to ask and present during class.

STEPS TO "OUTSMART" YOUR PROFESSORS IN THE CLASSROOM SETTING

1. **Brief and outline.** To begin with, when reading through your text, always brief and outline the main issues, facts, holding, and court reasoning. Professors will always ask students for the essentials of each case covered in the reading. Thus, this is a good point to begin when trying to foretell potential questions that may arise. If you brief your cases in an organized and efficient manner, you will already have answers to the first set of questions the professor will ask.

2. **Find the arguments.** Next, highlight and pull the main arguments from each litigant in the case. Every case will have at least one plaintiff and one defendant, sometimes even more. And each side will have their own set of arguments and justifications as to why they should win the case. Professors will generally focus on these arguments and it is essential to understand both the arguments and the reasons why they succeeded or failed.

3. **Review questions.** After pulling the main issues and arguments from each case, focusing on any review questions within the text will greatly serve your cause. Professors teach from the text and base their classroom questions and even many of their exam questions on the review questions presented after many of the cases in the text. After you have read and outlined your cases, take a few minutes to go through each question and write down the answer in your case briefs or the tabs in your book. Not only will you be prepared to answer the professor's questions, but you will also exude confidence and efficiency by having the answers organized right in front of your eyes.

4. **Use your resources.** Another easy step you can take to "outsmart" your professors is using case briefs and outlines. Let me remind you again that these should never replace your nightly reading or case briefs. However, they can be very helpful study aids to plan answers to potential questions. Many of these study guides will have topic-specific questions bringing to the surface specific issues or potential gray areas. These gray areas (that which does not fit nicely into a specific category or

yes/no answer) are favorites of law school professors. The black and white usually deal with black letter law and fit nicely into a definite yes or no. However, gray areas are "tweeners" (as in "in between two areas") and certainly the most challenging and thought-provoking questions. These will be all over the place on exams and extremely hard to answer. However, reviewing study aids will push you toward thought-provoking analysis and allow you to face these problems head on in the comfort of your own home so when it is time to duel with the professors, you will be properly trained.

5. **Pay attention.** A final step you can take to prepare for tough classroom questions is to pay attention in class. This is helpful for two reasons (among every other imaginable reason discussed throughout this book). First, each one of your professors has a unique teaching style and conducts classroom sessions in a distinct way. By paying attention to your professors, you will begin to understand and map the way class progresses. By gaining this insight, you will be able to preemptively plan to answer questions that are presented during each class. Professors are creatures of habit and will present each case in a similar way each time. That being said, paying attention will, at the least, allow you some insight into what to expect the next time you are called on. Furthermore, paying attention in class will allow you to plan ahead for upcoming questions. Scanning ahead in the material and finding the answer to potential questions before a professor calls on you is extremely beneficial, as you will have the answers at your fingertips as you get called on, instead of fumbling for the answers when you are on the spot. There is nothing more rewarding than beginning to answer a question as the professor finishes asking it—both to you and to the professor.

While all of these helpful tips will make your life as a student significantly easier, the best approach to succeeding with your professors is to stand out and make yourself an asset to them. By doing this, you offer your professors something extremely valuable, whether it be the correct answer or an insightful and thought-provoking statement. Through your involvement and preparation in class, you eliminate the times when you will be arbitrarily called on. Thus, when you raise your hand to participate, the professor will know, based on previous experiences, that you will offer a quality comment or answer and he or she will call on you to participate. Through this involvement, when it is time to call on students to answer questions, professors will be less inclined to look your way, because they know you will participate and add meaningful commentary when you are prepared to do so.

Contact Your Profs (Using Their Office Hours)

There will be many situations and instances when you will need to meet with your professors outside of class. Professors are very receptive to catering to student's schedules, questions, and concerns.

Common Reasons to Contact Your Professors During Office Hours
    Questions and concerns about course material
    Questions about classroom topics and issues
    Questions about the course syllabus
    Exam questions
    Paper questions
    Attendance issues
    Advice on exam preparation
    Advice on exam performance
    Overall law school concerns

 **sider's Guide**

Attorney Advice

Attorney Nick Goldberg of Greenberg Traurig says, "I found that students attending their professor's office hours can be helpful. If you are genuinely interested or confused with a particular course topic, go and show an avid interest as it can only help if the professor sees you on a regular basis, rather than two weeks before the final. While all law schools claim all grading is completely anonymous and blind, if you believe that you are too naive for the legal field."

While this list is comprehensive, it is surely not complete. There are endless issues, comments, questions, and concerns that will naturally arise as you travel through your first-year courses. Your professors are one of your most useful resources, and it is only to your advantage to use them liberally.

Advantages to Meeting with Your Professors
  Creating strong personal relationships with professors
  Receiving direct answers to complicated questions
  Clarifying any confusion concerning assignments and other syllabus issues

Professors wear many hats. When they are in class, they are a firm and strong professor presenting the information in a challenging and thought-provoking way. However, when professors are sitting in their offices outside of the classroom, they wear a different hat. Professors put down their guard and open up to students. This will allow you an opportunity to create a personal relationship based on common interests, not solely on law school. While this may not have a direct impact on grading or scores, as they are anonymous, professors will be more willing to help you with job searches and recommendations.

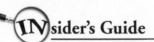 **sider's Guide**

Student Counsel

3L Rena Seidler says, "Concerning recommendation letters, don't ask professors for a recommendation letter simply because you did well in their class. While such a letter might be good, a great letter will come from a professor who knows you and who has heard you voice your thoughts, ideas, and opinions consistently in her class."

How to Get the Most Out of the Time You Spend with Your Professors

Contacting your profs. While e-mailing your professors may be the most efficient way to get in touch with them, spending a few minutes before or after class is the most direct way. Speaking to them face to face will allow you a direct opportunity to schedule a meeting and avoid most of the back and forth that may coincide with repetitious e-mails and correspondence. Another direct route for days when you do not have class is to call your professor's office. All contact information should be available on the course syllabus, and speaking on the phone to your professor is direct, quick, and easy.

Schedule the meeting. Once you have contacted your professor, the next step is picking a mutually convenient time to meet. Professors are extremely busy and do not have a lot of time outside of their normal office hours, so always try to meet them during their office hours. Check your course syllabus and see if their office hours fit into your schedule. If not, present your professor with a few other times that you can meet. Professors will generally be on campus before and after class, so take this into consideration and try to make appointments coinciding with class schedules.

Come prepared. Once you have set up your meeting with your professor, it is time to prepare for your meeting. If you come to a meeting unprepared, you will not only embarrass yourself, but you will also waste your professor's time. Prepare specific questions and thoughtful comments about course materials. This is an opportunity to receive direct feedback and answers to your tough questions. If you are confused about a specific topic, cite the point of your confusion, which will better allow the professor to guide you to a clear understanding of the material.

Say thank you. Be polite, courteous, and show your appreciation that your professor took time out of her busy schedule to meet with you. A simple e-mail soon after your meeting will certainly suffice and leave a lasting impression of your character and sincerity.

The value of face-to-face meetings with your professors cannot be stressed enough. These meetings allow you to create a strong personal relationship, quickly eliminate confusion that may arise from course material, enter into thoughtful conversations, and gain insight into exam preparation and finding success in your first year.

Networking Through Professors

Professors lead to opportunities. The biggest doors in law school are opened through the networks and resources of your professors. When I took sports law, I made a concerted effort to meet with my professor, participate in the class, and create a strong relationship. This strong relationship led to a summer clerkship opportunity, an independent study, and multiple networking opportunities with professional sports teams, agents, and some of the most successful attorneys in the field of sports law.

Professors are one of the strongest resources you will have at your fingertips. In addition to their ability to increase your chances for success through their knowledge, experience, and understanding of the course material, they are also powerful resources when it comes to your internships, summer clerkships, and ultimately, employment after law school.

Many professors will have endless connections and multiple networks comprising powerful and successful attorneys who work at all types of firms in all areas of law. Most of your professors will specialize in certain course topics and have vast knowledge and connections within these realms. Thus, your employment law professor will have previously worked at a great employment law firm and know all of the attorneys and partners within this firm. Your personal relationships with these professors will lead to multiple opportunities to cut through much of the job chase and have the opportunity, through your professors' efforts, to meet some of the most influential attorneys in your area of interest.

There are many obvious advantages to using your professors and their vast networks as a resource, not the least of which is the ease and efficiency of the entire process. Look at the cost versus reward analysis alone. Contacting your professors and discussing potential contacts they may have or potential job openings they may know of could lead to a prosperous career. Just a few minutes and a few questions are certainly worth the potential rewards, whether they be a great summer clerkship or a heartfelt recommendation letter.

sider's Guide

Student Counsel

3L Justin Goodman says, "Professors have connections everywhere. If you need help and you have earned their respect, they will go out of their way to help you make connections and find jobs. If you are interested in a particular subject matter, ask the professor of that subject if he needs a research assistant. It is a great writing experience. Furthermore, you may even have a chance to get paid, and your interaction with the professor gains you an ally in your future job search and other plans. Don't be afraid of your professors—treat them with respect, but they are real people just like you."

Steps to Take When Asking a Professor to Help with Jobs

Step One: *Schedule a meeting.* Contact your professors via e-mail or approach them before or after class in a respectful and appreciative manner and find a mutually convenient time to meet.

Step Two: *Plan ahead.* Once you have scheduled a meeting with your professor, it is time to plan ahead. Find specific law firms in which you are interested and write down the names and partners of each firm. When you meet with your professor, ask specific questions about these firms and find out if your professors know any of the partners. If you are looking for a recommendation letter or something of that nature, bring your resume and plan on talking about yourself for a bit so the professor will have the chance to get to know you better. Creating a strong personal relationship before you ask for a recommendation letter will serve your interests best, as professors will be more willing to comply with your requests and will also be in a better position to do so.

Step Three: *Take notes.* Always come prepared with a notepad and pen so you can take down any pertinent information you may receive. Your professors may feel comfortable giving you contact information from their network and allowing you the opportunity to contact them directly.

Step Four: *Follow up with your new contacts.* If you are fortunate enough to receive contact information from your professors, the next step is to follow up with your new contacts. Before you ever call an attorney, do your research and come prepared. Find out what firm she works for, who her clients are, what areas of law she practices, and her personal background, such as her education. If you are serious about working for someone you are contacting, then you are interviewing them as well to make sure this is a good opportunity and a beneficial situation for you.

Step Five: *Thank your professors.* Always show your appreciation toward anyone who helped you along the way. Sending e-mails should be the bare minimum; extend yourself and put forth a little more effort, because it goes a long way. Take just a few extra minutes after you meet with your professors and send them a handwritten thank-you letter. It is a relatively small and inconsequential gesture, but these are the types of gestures that make all the difference in the professional world, because they leave lasting impressions of your character and morals.

Taking time out of your busy schedule during the course of your first year to meet with your professors to utilize their vast networks can have limitless effects on your professional life and even secure a wonderful clerkship or future job opportunity. Professors are on your side and are willing to help you in any way that they can so long as you are respectful, appreciative, and diligent with your classroom participation and efforts.

Parents, Friends, and Family

It will not be uncommon for your professors to be close friends, family, or your parents. Attorneys are an interesting breed in the sense that they have humongous networks, connections, and relationships. Thus, it will not be uncommon to enter law school and have a concurrent personal relationship with one of your professors.

When you are faced with such an issue, alleviate your needless worrying by approaching the professor on the first day of class and discussing your personal relationships. Law school professors are extremely professional and conduct themselves in a respectful manner at all times. They will not give you special treatment. They will check the personal relationships at the classroom door and so should you. The woman standing at the front of the classroom is not your friend or your cousin. She is your educator and your advocate. Communication is the best step to take to create a productive and beneficial environment without any awkward experiences.

Sick/Personal Days

A final note about your etiquette when dealing with your professors concerns sick and personal days. On your first day of class, you will receive a syllabus outlining the attendance policy for each one of your courses. Read through this meticulously and ingrain it into your memory.

Many professors have specific policies concerning religious holidays and deaths in the family. While they may not be outlined in the syllabus, it is important to speak to the professor early on and find out exactly which absences she will excuse and which she will not. Furthermore, many schools have specific policies concerning religious holidays and deaths in the family. These policies are extremely important, as all professors and faculty must follow them. Always remember that your professors are human and care about not only your education, but also your well-being. They will be understanding and sympathetic toward situations you face in your life.

However, while some professors are very concerned with your excuses and reasons for not attending class, some simply do not care about your attendance and the justifications for your absences. It is essential to be malleable and react accordingly to each one of your professors. To be safe, however, contact all your professors via a short e-mail to let them know that you will not be in class and give them your reason. This way, you will be sure to find out each professor's preference regarding absences.

Let the Synergy Begin

Professors have a limitless amount of power over and influence on your success as a law school student and ultimately as an attorney. This chapter is just another example of synergy. Each one of these small steps alone may not have a huge impact on your law school success, but when taking into account each meticulous detail and implementing them into your daily routine, you will come across as an organized, responsible, and respectful student—the type of student professors would be happy to recommend to their network of friends as a wonderful employee.

CHAPTER FOUR

Filling the Rolodex: Networking During Your First Year

JANUARY 25, 2004

My Classmates

"Get to know your classmates." It went through my head again and again. The first class of my second semester of law school and I still think back to my first day when our professor adamantly pleaded with us to "get to know our classmates." I made a concerted effort early on to get to know my classmates. One thing I have learned in law school is that professors don't waste your time. If they are repetitious about a fact, statement, or issue, it is important and you should follow their direction. So I had this great idea to compile as many AOL screen names as possible so I could chat during class and discuss pertinent legal issues the professor was covering. It also helped to have the answer to the question flash on my screen when I was obviously fishing for the answer. While chatting away in class with a close friend, he decides to tell me the funniest joke I have ever heard. Seriously, this joke could have been the centerpiece in the comedic hall of fame. The headliner in a good flick. Or even the last-second buzzer beater in the championship game. In the middle of our discussion of contracts, this comedic masterpiece pops up on my screen. Not knowing exactly what it is, I read it and begin laughing hysterically in the middle of class. This draws a slight amount of attention my way, and the professor turns to me and says, "Mr. Spizman, I didn't realize I was such a comedian. What is so funny?" Knowing exactly what just happened, my friend begins laughing hysterically, and the professor looks in his direction, knowing immediately what has just transpired. He turns to me, then back to my friend, and says, "Lets keep the inside jokes outside of class." I guess this wasn't exactly what my professor meant when he said "get to know your classmates." But hey, I do the best I can—sometimes my timing is just a little off.

Let the Networking Begin

You will make good friends, great friends, and even best friends as you journey through your first year. These friends will turn into networking opportunities as you become an attorney and adventure through your legal career. Your first-year classmate will one day be a state court judge presiding over one of your insurance fraud cases; your study group partner will be the prosecuting attorney in a criminal case where you are representing the defendant; and the student who helped you with an outline for an upcoming exam may end up being your partner in a successful law firm. Get to know everyone and stay in touch because you can't foretell the future and they may end up being key contacts in the legal community.

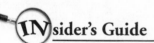 **IN**sider's Guide

Attorney Advice

Attorney Nick Goldberg says, "Networking should be done at all times: At bars, at dinners, through family, at law school, etc. It never hurts to be in a normal conversation with someone and mention that you are in law school. They will almost certainly respond that a friend, relative, or acquaintance of some sort is an attorney and they would · love to introduce you to her. Always remember to follow up with whomever you talk to and keep up with them if you make a good connection. You never know when that individual will be the gateway to a great opportunity in the future."

Lifelines

It's as simple as this: When you enter law school, your classmates are in the same exact boat as you. They are your lifelines, your support systems, and each one of them offers a unique opportunity. Whether it is a study group, a networking opportunity, a study guide, or anything and everything in between, your classmates are one of the most underused and underrated keys to success in law school. The most successful students in law school are the ones who use the resources available to them in the most effective and efficient way. While I don't condone looking at people as nothing more than resources, never forget that each student occupying a seat in your first-year courses has the possibility of offering you a unique opportunity. Consider a student who desperately wants to break into employment law. She is not sure exactly how to do so and really has no connections in the industry. One day over lunch she strikes up a conversation with one of her classmates and he starts complaining about how all he wants to do is be an entertainment attorney but his father is upset he won't follow in his footsteps and take over his employment law firm. Yhatzee. Bingo. Blackjack. Call it whatever you want, a door just opened for this first-year law student and if she networks appropriately and maintains a relationship with her new friend, she may find herself sitting in front of his father discussing job opportunities. Use your lifelines and network your resources, as this will only help you find success in your journey through your first year of law school.

Breaking the Ice with Your Classmates

Networking with your classmates sounds easy enough, but situations such as these are always easier said than done. Fortunately, there are many steps you can take during your first year to meet your classmates, make new friends, and network your new resource.

Be Polite

The easiest way to scare people off is to be rude. Always have a smile on your face and be kind to your classmates. It is easy sometimes to get lost in the shuffle of law school and close yourself off to your classmates and even be short with them, because the first year is an extremely stressful time. But remember that they are there to help you, and they are experiencing the same anxiety and stress that you are. If misery loves company, then just look around at your classmates and join in the fun. There will be times when you will be rude by accident. However, always be quick to apologize and explain why you are being short with your classmate. She might have the answer to your stress and even be able to help you with your problem.

Find Common Ground

Your classmates will have various backgrounds and widespread interests outside of law school. Some of them might be avid sports fans, shoppers, musicians, movie snobs, pet lovers, etc. If you talk to your classmates you will get to know them better and find that they have some of the same interests that you do. Use these interests as conversation starters and opportunities to get to know your classmates better. If nothing else, you can share a brief distraction with them. I would often take a glance at my neighbors' computers to see what they were surfing on the Web. Most often they were not surfing law blogs, but rather checking their fantasy scores, a new line of denim, or anything and everything in between. This will give you a gauge of their interests and, while I don't condone snooping, a glance at *www.CNN.com* on their computer won't hurt anyone.

Show Interest

Once you have found common ground with your classmates, show interest in their lives. Talk to them about their interests and their "out of class lives." Showing interest in others is the quickest way to become close friends and grasp many of the networking opportunities by the horns. Find out what your classmates' parents do, where they are from, and where they live. Besides, everyone knows that people love talking about themselves more than anything else in the world.

Get Their Contact Info

What good is a contact that you cannot reach? Offer your e-mail address and phone numbers to your classmates and always try to get theirs if they are willing to offer them to you. This will allow you to call them when you have questions about class or assignments. Phone calls and e-mails make things more personal and create a sense of value in a relationship, creating a stronger resource and networking opportunity for you and your friends.

Get in Touch

Make plans. If you are going out for a drink with your friends or going to see a movie, invite your classmates along. The easiest way to get to know your classmates is outside of the law school environment. Students put their guard down more readily and are more willing to open up and get to know you while also allowing you an inside track to their lives.

These are all very easy to implement in your law school schedule, as they take little time and effort. Besides, you are spending so many days and nights at law school that you might as well get to know your bunkmates.

When Should I Network?

While networking with your classmates during your first year is extremely valuable, there are vast resources outside of your class-mates, including attorneys, professors, and visitors to your law school. Focus on every available means to networking. As with any resource, there is an optimal time and place to use your network-ing opportunities in order to maximize your success with this skill. From orientation through first-year exams, networking opportuni-ties will always be available for the most entrepreneurial students each and every day of law school.

Attorney Advice

Attorney Jeff Solomon says, "Networking is about meeting the people you don't know, but should know. I did not get my job through friends or family, but rather through friends of friends, the people that I had heard of only in passing. Quite often friends introduce you to people, and you quickly forget their name, or who they are. These introductions are the first step in finding a new job or creating new opportunities. It is this extended circle of friends that allows you to expand your current roster of contacts and increase your likelihood of finding the right opportunity. The next time you go out, take time to talk to everyone and treat each person the same. You never know if they can, and will, help you. My best advice for networking is to reach out to people outside of your immediate circle of friends, outside of your comfort zone. By taking that first step, you will be amazed at how many opportunities will fall into your lap."

The Most Valuable Times in Which to Network While on Campus

Orientation. Orientation is a wonderful time to begin networking with your classmates because everyone is in the same exact boat. As the semester progresses, you will find students closing themselves off and spending their time with a chosen few for whatever reasons. However, during orientation, very few students know one another and most students are willing to open up to their classmates. Take this opportunity and introduce yourself to everyone. Ask them: Where did you go to college? Where are you from? And, Why in the world did you decide to attend law school? You will find that your classmates will be particularly receptive to such questions and that they will be happy to strike up a conversation with you. Use this unique and novel situation to create an invaluable network for your first day of law school.

Classes. Follow "the fifteen-minute rule." Throughout law school I had a blanket rule to always get to class fifteen minutes early so I had the opportunity to talk to my classmates, "shoot the shit," and get to know them. This is a great time to network because the students are pretty relaxed and receptive to talking about what exactly is going on in their lives. Ask them about the reading last night, the assignment for the next class, or even what they did the previous evening. Catch them on a Monday, and you can talk to them about their weekend activities. Use these fifteen minutes as an opportunity to catch up with everyone in your class and create potential networks for future use.

Lunch. Lunch is one of the best times to network. Most law schools will have a common area where students can spend time between classes and eat their lunch. There will also be a cafeteria at school and numerous restaurants surrounding most campuses. This is a great time to relax and spend time with your classmates. Invite friends to lunch, invite strangers to lunch, and invite yourself to lunch. Furthermore, during these lunches, many law schools will have club meetings. Whether it is the Federalist Society or the Juvenile Law Organization, attend these meetings to meet students with the same interests as you, and this will be your most useful network out there.

Finals. Surprisingly enough, finals time is a great time to network with classmates for the sole reason that almost every student will be on campus at all times of the day. You will see your friends, your classmates, and people you didn't even know were in your classes. Take this opportunity to take study breaks, snack breaks, drink breaks, and anything and everything else in between to talk to your classmates. Ask them what they are studying and if they are interested in the subject. This is a great way to gauge whether they have similar interests and would be useful in your network.

Office hours. Although mentioned in the above chapters, it bears reiterating that a wonderful time to network is during your professors' office hours. First and foremost, this is one of the few times you will have the full attention of the professor in a controlled setting without the pressures and formalities of a classroom. Secondly, remember that your professors are attorneys first. They are successful attorneys and generally specialize in a particular area of the law. They surely have endless contacts and networking opportunities available to those students who put forth the effort and show interest in their area of practice and expertise. Professors are very approachable and generally accept positions at a university to help students as well as teach them. While your professors will always have great networks and connections, they will only be able to help so many students find a job in a particular area of interest. The early bird gets the worm. Start early and you may just find that a wonderful opportunity is staring you right in the eye every day of class.

Law School Organizations. Almost every day of law school, a specific group will make arrangements to bring a prestigious attorney on campus to speak to their members. For example, during my second year of law school, I was vice president of the Sports Law Society. We brought sports agents and sports law attorneys to campus to speak to our members. In an industry as cutthroat as the sports business, it was extremely valuable for our members to have a direct path to speak to an agent with actual NFL clients. Just by attending a lunch meeting, you can receive a free lunch (which is quite valuable when you have loan money to repay) and an opportunity to network with a successful attorney. One hour of your time every week can lead to monumental success in your networking. Take full advantage of these quick networking opportunities, because they are one of the easiest ways to find a meaningful prospect.

Speakers. In addition to group lunch meetings, many times the university will bring in speakers to speak to the college of law. After these meetings there are usually receptions where the speakers mingle with law students and discuss anything and everything in a casual and relaxed atmosphere. Attend these lectures and take a few minutes to go to the receptions afterward. Many times these speakers will specialize in a particular area of the law, and if this particular area is of interest to you, chat with them for a few minutes and express your interest in their field. Ask for their card and see if they have an opportunity to meet with you in the near future. They will almost certainly agree to help you however they can. Always remember that these attorneys were in the same spot as you at some point in their legal career and they remember how they benefited from the help of others. They will be happy to help you in any way that they can.

Visitors. On many occasions, alumni of the law school will drop in to visit their alma mater. They will be curious to see how the school has changed and will be more than willing to talk to students about their time at the university. Seize this opportunity and offer to show them around the law school and talk about your experiences. You never know if they are a successful judge, litigator, or specialized attorney. Whatever the case, they will be more than happy to talk to you and help you in any way that they can. This is an easy way to expand your network. Alumni of your college of law are already in your network of accessible people; it is just up to you to reach out and become part of theirs.

Career Services Office. Every law school across the country has some form of a career services office. This can be a useful tool for networking, as this office's sole responsibility is to find you a job. They have books filled with attorneys and employment opportunities and are happy to make calls, distribute your resume, and aid in your job search. They are a direct pathway to a large and resourceful network. It may be helpful to set up a meeting early on and check back on a regular basis to find job openings and networking opportunities. Your school's career services office will often post flyers about legal events around the state and region. Needless to say, this is a wonderful networking opportunity, as a large group of attorneys specializing in a particular area of law will be together discussing current issues and events in the field. Use your career services office as a direct and resourceful tool to building an effective network early on in your legal career.

Organizing Your Network

Now that we have a network in place, let's talk about the most effective and efficient ways to use this powerful resource. The power of a network cannot be understated. Students often overlook networking throughout law school, but it is definitely one of the easiest ways to set up future jobs, find opportunities, and gain valuable contacts. Networks grow both exponentially and quickly. Imagine a spider web with one of your classmates in the middle. The web is woven at an unreal pace with your friend's network becoming your network and so on and so forth. By the end of it all, you may receive an interview, a job offer, or valuable guidance from an individual four degrees removed from your original source, all by maintaining a strong relationship with your original classmate.

A valuable network is one that you use on a regular basis. This can be a little overwhelming based on the size of your network and the opportunities available through your network. However, it is quite manageable if you stay focused and follow these easy steps.

First of all, it is imperative to stay organized and maintain your network. You cannot use your network if it is not organized. Imagine going to the biggest mall in the world. As you walk in, you are told you just won the grand-prize giveaway for the month—a free one-hour shopping spree. You have one hour to grab as much as you can, and whatever you can get your hands on is yours for the taking: every designer store, every brand, every product you could ever imagine. While you are overwhelmed by your luck, you begin to plot out your course of attack. The first thing you do when you walk into this consumer's dream is grab a map and organize your shopping route. You would not simply look at a list of stores and begin frantically running through the mall. The same is true with a network. You do not simply make your contacts, look through your network, and pat yourself on the back for all your hard work. Rather, you stay focused, map out your contacts, and create a plan of attack. Your network is like a list of stores in the mall scenario. They do you no good unless you use them as a map for your point of attack. A successful end may be our goal, but the means is what will guide us there. Without a strong networking plan and organization, your network is nothing more than a list of names.

So the question remains, how do I stay organized with my growing list of contacts?

Ways to Get Organized

Write things down. Once you make a new connection or extend your network, at the least, write down your new contact's name, phone numbers, and e-mail address. This will give you a quick reference guide to the individual's information. Using a resource such as Microsoft Outlook, your e-mail system's personal organizer, a

PDA, Smartphone, or a good old-fashioned pen and address book will be very helpful. Once you have the time, try answering the following questions and add the answers to your contact's quick reference guide:

What does your contact do for a living?

Who is your contact's employer? What firm does your contact work for?

How did you meet the contact?

When is your contact's birthday?

What are your contact's interests?

Document your conversations. Throughout your networking, you will have multiple conversations and encounters with your contacts. Whenever you speak to them on the phone or bump into them at the courthouse or at school, go to your quick reference guide and document these occurrences. In your quick reference guide, write down the date, where you saw them, and what the two of you talked about. Law students live a busy life, talk to a lot of people, and are scatterbrained at times. However, if you give yourself a play-by-play of the time you spend with your contacts, you will always be on top of your game and always be able to track the history you have with particular contacts. Besides, if you can't illustrate your organization with your contacts, why would they hire you or recommend you to anyone in their network?

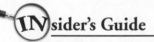 **sider's Guide**

Attorney Advice

Attorney Nick Goldberg says, "I found my e-mail system at school to be rather difficult and burdensome. I decided to take my home e-mail and use it as my primary e-mail for school. I changed it online via the school (to have e-mails automatically forwarded to my home account) so I did not have to check two e-mail accounts and could always document any conversations I had with my contacts or between me and the school. It made it so much easier to have that readily available at my fingertips."

Use your e-mail. E-mail is the easiest way to document your conversations. An e-mail site like Gmail never deletes your e-mails. They simply archive your e-mails as conversations. These conversations are stored on their huge network (pun intended) and are easily accessible whenever you need them. All you have to do is search for keywords in the e-mail, such as the recipients address or topic and you will be able to reference entire conversations you may have had months ago with your contacts. Be careful when using your law school's e-mail system, because many of them use servers that do not document past e-mails and, once deleted, old messages are gone forever.

Using Your Network

After you feel comfortable with the organization of your network, you are ready to take the next step in effectively using your network. Using your contacts is never something you should force, as there is no reason to use an ace in the hole when you are drawing dead (excuse the poker slang). Begin by listing all of your contacts and taking a look at the big picture. What exactly do you need at this point? A job? Job guidance? Advice? Information for law school? Once you have answered these relatively easy questions, you can truly hone your contacts and network appropriately. Each one of your contacts will be a valuable resource for one reason or another, and it is your job to decide exactly which contacts fill your needs at that time. Many of them will offer specific help, whether it be a job offer, assisting with an independent study, or putting you in touch with one of their colleagues. This is part of the reason why you should document previous conversations with your contacts.

Contact your network directly via phone, as this shows interest and is more professional. Most of these attorneys and professors receive tons of e-mails a day and the last thing you want is for your e-mail to get lost in the bunch or accidentally deleted. More times than not, you will be in touch with your contact's secretary. Get to know her. Introduce yourself when you initially contact her and be extremely friendly and polite. She is the gatekeeper and has a large amount of control over your contact's life and the messages she gets and those that may be lost in translation. When speaking to your contact's secretary and leaving a message, specify who you are and make sure she knows that you previously met with her employer and she recommended that you call if you ever needed anything. Not to be dubious of secretaries, but it only helps if you make a connection with them and relay the importance of hearing back from the boss.

sider's Guide

Student Counsel

2L Jerimiah Jarmin says, "Occasionally you will be lucky enough and your contacts will give you a direct line or cell phone number. Always use this number and contact them directly, as it ensures they will get your message and hopefully contact you as soon as they have a free moment. When you initially meet with your contacts, try your hardest to get a direct line or a cell phone number. Certain attorneys do not spend a lot of time in the office and it can be extremely tough to get in touch with them, because they are always on the run."

Once you get in touch with your contact, the opportunity to use her resources begins. Most attorneys are extremely busy and their time is rather valuable. Therefore, when you contact people in your network, be very specific, be very quick on the phone, and prepare ahead of time. Decide exactly what you are hoping to get from the conversation before the conversation even begins. Jot down notes and questions to ask your contact so you stay focused and do not take more of their time than needed. When preparing for the conversation with your contact, always have a pen and piece of paper handy in case they give you phone numbers and names of people with whom to get in touch.

If your contacts do in fact give you names and numbers of their colleagues, enter them into your contact reference guide immediately. Give your initial contacts some time to get in touch with their colleagues so they can let their friends know you will be calling in the near future. It may even be beneficial to e-mail your new contact and introduce yourself, attach your resume, and ask her if there is a good time to get in touch and speak for a few minutes. Try to be flexible with your schedule so she can make time for you when she has a few minutes.

Tips to Ensure You Leave a Lasting Impression

Overdress. Perception is nine-tenths of the law. We are what we are perceived to be. Dress professionally for your meetings, as it exudes professionalism and maturity. You should enter your meetings with your contact and be the best-dressed individual in the room. Dress as if you are arguing in front of the Supreme Court. There is no downside to overdressing. I once went into an interview with a contact from my network. My parents put me in touch with an Atlanta-based attorney specializing in criminal defense and entertainment law. I was extremely excited to meet with him because I heard he was a wonderful attorney, a great guy, and he specialized in an area of law that interested me. I walked into his office and said, "Mr. Cohen, it is a pleasure to meet you. Thank you for taking time out of your busy schedule to meet with me." He looked at me blankly, wearing a pair of slacks and an unbuttoned shirt, and said, "Justin, my father's name is Mr. Cohen, and take that damn tie and jacket off." I thought he was kidding, but it turned out he wouldn't even begin speaking to me until I followed his directions. He offered me a job soon after and he is one of many great contacts and friends I have in the city.

Be polite. As obvious as it may seem, being polite will get you everywhere. You were raised a certain way, so do your parents' hard work justice and use the manners you were taught. Always refer to your contacts with the appropriate title, whether it be Mr., Mrs., or Ms. Let them tell you to call them by something other than their last name. Always say please and thank you and maintain eye contact.

Be early. Whenever you have an initial meeting with a contact, always be the one waiting. An attorney should never have to wait on you to do you a favor. Print out directions to your contact's office, look through them the night before, and if you are unfamiliar with the area or do not know exactly how to get there, leave fifteen minutes early to ensure you do not get lost. Always bring cash for parking, as many attorneys work in large office buildings with parking decks. Finally, always compensate for traffic if you are traveling across town in the morning or afternoon in a big city. Even during lunchtime, there will be a highway crunch, so make sure to give yourself extra time to prevent tardiness.

Talk to the secretary. Never forget how much power an attorney's secretary may have. If he likes you, he will find time to work you into your contact's schedule and hopefully put in a good word for you. More often than not, you will be spending most of your time on the phone with your contact's secretary anyway, so be polite, ask him questions about himself, and thank him for all his help.

Ask questions. The most sure-fire way to get to know a contact is to ask personal questions. Always start with the easy ones: Where are you from? Where did you go to undergrad? Law school? How did you get where you are today? What are your future goals? Attorneys love talking about themselves and this is an easy way to get to know a contact. I cannot stress enough how important it is to show interest in not only your contact, but in her career as well. Showing a strong interest in her area of practice will only give her another reason to help you or even hire you.

The three Ps. When you have the opportunity to meet with your contacts, always come prepared with the three Ps: pen, paper, and personals. Pens and paper are self-explanatory, but personals include your personal statement, your personal writing sample, and your personal resume. Almost every attorney, professor, or real-world contact you meet with will ask you for your personal resume, if not a personal writing sample as well. Always have extra copies of the third P in case your contact wants to forward them to colleagues, friends, or coworkers.

Follow up. Always follow up with your contacts and express your appreciation for their time. Whenever I get back to my apartment after an interview, I quickly send my contact an e-mail thanking her for her time and effort earlier in the day. I then wait a week and send her a thank-you letter. I like to let a little time pass before I send out a thank-you letter because when an attorney receives it a few weeks after meeting with you, it keeps your meeting and your personality fresh in his or her mind.

This may be a lot of nitpicky information to follow, but successful networking comes down to your attention to details. Imagine a networking opportunity as a courtship between a man and a woman. In the initial stages, you get to know each other and take it slow. As things heat up, you have the opportunity to spend more time with that person, obtain more information from her, and ask her to help you out more and more. By the time it is all over, you have a strong relationship, talk with and see each other regularly, and mutually benefit from your interactions. While I am not condoning dating your contacts, treat your new relationship with them as a courtship and be on your best behavior, take good care of them, and pay attention to the little things, because that translates to successful relationships and successful networks.

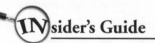

(IN)sider's Guide

Attorney Advice

Attorney Jordan Cohen says, "Interviewing and networking boil down to the small things. Everyone deserves to be in the interview and deserves to be in front of the hiring partner, but it is those interviewees that take the extra steps and leave a lasting impression that get ahead. Always print your resume on resume paper, as well as any other documents that you plan to give your contact, as it adds a nice touch of professionalism and class. Dress well, be on time, and always express your gratitude for their efforts."

Once your network is organized, it is important to maintain your network on a regular basis. Many of the people in your network are extremely busy and work hard. That being said, it is easy for them to forget a previous meeting, phone conversation, or offer to help your job search. To avoid such problems, contact the attorneys and professors in your network on a regular basis. Whether it is to discuss a legal issue, ask for advice, or just to say hello, these quick check-ins via e-mail or telephone act as refreshers for the busy folks in your network.

The Power of a Network

Keeping yourself organized and maintaining contact with your network will serve you greatly. These simple steps will allow you to use your network to its fullest extent. Just to illustrate the power of a law student's network, enjoy these examples from real students who benefited greatly from their own personal networks:

Attorney Justin Goodman says, "I found that the best networking tool was to always let my professors know what interested me. During my second year, I discussed my potential options for a summer internship with my professors. One of them knew an attorney at one of the potential job sites, put me in contact with them directly, and even followed up himself. In the end, I got the job and a great addition to my growing network. Furthermore, look for help in unexpected places. When a friend or family member meets a member of the legal community and mentions you, follow up if the person offers to help. After a meeting with one such attorney, they introduced me to another person that ended up giving me a job."

Attorney Nick Goldberg says, "I got my job at a large firm through networking with a close friend from law school. His mother went to high school with a lawyer at my firm, which eventually helped me get a job here. I had been rejected from my firm numerous times, but when I sent my resume to my friend's mother, I got an interview and she put in a good word for me. After my interviews at the firm, they offered me the job on the spot. It is truly amazing what a little insider action can do!"

Attorney Neera Makwana says, "Since I'm new to Atlanta, networking got me everywhere. I made an effort to send my resume out to big firms on my own during my first year of law school. Even though this resulted in a lot of rejections (because I accidentally sent out my resume *after* recruiting season was over), one law firm in particular invited me to have lunch with them despite the fact that they were no longer hiring. This helped me establish a relationship with the law firm early on in my law school career. I am now working for that firm."

3L Tom Devine says, "Networking provided me with a very unique opportunity. Through networking with friends, I found out one of my old college buddies was studying in China and had a great connection at a prestigious law firm out there. I contacted him and he got me a job offer, and I moved to China for a year to learn Mandarin and work for the law firm. Not only was it great for my resume, but I can get my foot in the door in any international law firm because of the networking I did early in my legal career."

Attorney Jeff Solomon says, "I found my job through a friend of mine's old fraternity brother that I barely knew. I had met him once or twice, and thought nothing of it. He seemed like a nice enough guy, but I didn't know him all that well. We were talking one day, when he offered to pass my resume along at the large firm in which he worked. None of my friends had offered me this, so why did he? The simple answer is that most people love to help other people, especially when it comes to their line of work. The key is to branch out and meet as many people as you can, because you never know who will help you along your path of finding the right opportunity. To date, I still work at that same firm."

3L Stacey Hornsby says, "I went to just about every event that special-interest professional law associations hosted. At one such event, the students were asked to stand up and be recognized for their accomplishments and scholastic endeavors. Then, the attorneys and judges present at the meeting were charged with helping the students with jobs, mentoring, guidance, etc. Afterward, several attorneys approached me with summer internship offers. If I hadn't networked through these meetings, I would never have gotten the summer internship offers that I did. I was one of the fortunate few; through my networking, I actually got to choose the right summer job for me."

Attorney Lino Rodriguez says, "I am currently working at a charitable organization practicing immigration law. The immigration community in my hometown is quite small and I was able to acquire my present position partly through references from individuals I had met at Hispanic Bar Association meetings, which

I attended regularly. While there I networked with speakers and anyone and everyone they brought in."

These are just a few examples of the power of networking. In each of these cases, the law students focused on their network and found a meaningful and useful way to find employment in their particular field of interest. There are hundreds of stories exactly like those mentioned here, in each and every law school across the country. There are also another hundred stories where a student interviewed at twenty different law firms and is still scouring the want ads for a job. The point is simple and the concept is powerful: Making just one phone call a day during the course of your first year of law school will amount to the creation of an endless network and ultimately the right clerkship or job for you. By no means am I trying to dissuade you from attending interviews and contacting potential employers; I am only trying to simplify your job search. One phone call or e-mail a day during your first year of law school will build a magnificent and vast network.

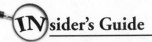 ## IN sider's Guide

Attorney Advice
Attorney Sarah Kass says, "Networking is probably the most important thing you can do in law school. You never know when a person you meet might be able to help you professionally. When you are looking for a job, meeting people and letting them know that you are looking for a job is imperative. Even if networking does not get you a job, the people you meet will likely be your peers and opposing counsel throughout your legal career."

Furthermore, in the world of law school, you encounter attorneys on an almost unimaginable level. Speakers at your law school, visitors from law firms, law school alumni, professors, and the occasional visitor are all at your fingertips on a daily basis. Each one of duce yourself, make a connection, grab a business card, or ask for advice. They offer themselves to the law school and its students in order to provide helpful advice and networking opportunities. It is not by chance or coincidence they are on campus chatting with students. These attorneys want to help and are happy to become part of your network. Remember that the pen is mightier than the sword, so grab your favorite writing utensil and write down the name and e-mail address of your network's newest addition.

The Etiquette of the Network

While adequate networking is the majority of the battle, do not forget your manners and proper etiquette when using your network. The fastest way to open a door is to network, but the quickest way to close a door is through poor etiquette. Previously I discussed the proper etiquette when meeting with attorneys in your network, but there are also some important etiquette tips to follow when initially approaching attorneys in hopes of adding them to your network.

FIVE RULES OF NETWORKING ETIQUETTE

1. **Be aware of the time.** Always look at your watch, figuratively speaking. The attorneys, professors, and colleagues in your network are busy people. There is always an appropriate time to network and use your network. Professors open up their offices regularly each and every week for students to come in and talk about anything and everything. Networking during office hours is better than after class, but both are valuable times to engage your professors. Be conscious of the attorneys in your network and try not to call a tax attorney two days before tax season ends, or a litigator during the course of a high-profile trial. Furthermore, be conscious of the amount of time you ask those people in your network to spend helping you. They gave you their e-mail and phone numbers for a reason, but if they feel you are overstepping your boundaries or taking advantage of their generosity, they will quickly close the door to their office, both figuratively and literally.

2. **Use your compass.** There is a time for networking and there is also a place. Use your compass, figuratively speaking. If an attorney is on campus to speak to a group of students, this is a potentially great time to network, because they are opening themselves up to the university and its students. However, if you run into an attorney after lunch and she is rushing to make a closing argument in court, she probably doesn't have much time to network at that point. Be patient, assertive, and attentive and you will always find an appropriate time to touch base and network in a useful manner. The last thing you want to do is rush through a networking opportunity, because you never get a second chance to make a first impression, and annoying an attorney before you even introduce yourself is not the most effective manner to effectively network.

3. **Don't forget how your mama raised ya.** She taught you to say please and thank you and follow up with people. She also taught you to be conscious of others' feelings and attentive to details. Use these childhood skills during your networking opportunities. Always be polite and always thank attorneys and professors for their time. Their time is valuable, and they are using billable hours to spend giving you advice and helping your future at their own personal expense. While they may not view it in that fashion, you should, as it will make you even more conscious of their time. Follow up with a thank-you letter a few days after your initial encounter. This will not only show your appreciation, but also keep your name fresh in their mental rolodex, which is filled to the brim as is. It is rather easy to send a quick email as you can do it anytime, but spending the time to write a letter a week later shows you are still thinking about your meeting and appreciate your contact's time and effort.

4. **Dress the part.** Always remember to dress the part. In this day and age, looking sharp sells well. If you look like an attorney, you will be treated like an attorney. Show respect to the individuals in your network by taking the meetings and encounters with them seriously and wearing a tie (for the guys) or a professional business suit if you are a woman. You

should strive to look as put together and organized as they do. If they have respect for your preparation, they will bend over backward to help you out. Besides, your mom would kill you if you showed up at a job interview wearing a pair of torn jeans and a basketball jersey.

5. **Be prepared.** It is an extremely simple concept, and it can be detrimental if you don't follow it. Before speaking to contacts in your network and especially before you meet with them, do your homework, literally. Research their education, accomplishments, and area of practice. By infusing your knowledge of their lives into a conversation with them, you show interest and attention to detail, in addition to illustrating that you come to your meetings prepared and take those meetings seriously.

Start Building that Network of Yours

Networking may be the most useful piece of the law school puzzle. During your stint as a first-year law student, you enter the legal community as a fetus. You are confused, surrounded by new people and experiences, and not exactly sure how to navigate the long road ahead. However, each day you will grow intellectually and figure out exactly how to circumvent the new puzzle that you face. Every day as a 1L will bring new challenges along with new opportunities. As mentioned previously, use these opportunities to the fullest extent and network every step of the way. Your grades may end up lower than expected; your spirits may need a slight uplift; and your mind may need a serious break. However, the one thing that should remain consistent and strong throughout your first year of law school is your network.

You will not have control over many pieces of law school, but you can control the output and the input of your network. If you choose to take opportunities and meet people in every situation imaginable, you will have an unbelievable network. However, if you slack off and overlook potential opportunities, your network will lack size and usefulness. Look to the examples given earlier. Each of the 1Ls discusses an opportunity that arose from networking. They did not discuss their grades, accomplishments, or awards as the means to their successful end. They discussed their networks and how their networks gave them a fine opportunity. Grades and accomplishments are extremely important and should never be overlooked even for a second, but the age-old tale will tell you that the hardest thing to do is get your foot in the door, and the easiest way to stop that door from closing is through adequate networking.

INsider's Guide

Student Counsel

3L Jerimiah Jarmin says, "It is extremely important to be friendly to everyone, because everyone knows one another in the legal field. Negativity associated with your name can hurt your prospects at landing a great internship or job. Word of mouth spreads quickly, and leaving a poor impression with even one attorney can spread across the always close-knit legal community and have an impact on a potential opportunity."

This chapter has focused on the value of a large and organized network. Furthermore, I have outlined the steps to network maintenance and proper etiquette when using your network. Finally, this chapter has presented real-life examples of how networking paid off considerably for first-year law students. I said it to begin this chapter and I would also like to end on this simple yet powerful note: Networking cannot be underestimated and can be the most direct and easiest way to find great opportunities, valuable summer experiences, and gainful employment after law school.

DECEMBER 3, 2003

Game Time

Well, it has been a fun ride. Attending class, reading a few pages a night, participating in discussions . . . this hasn't been so bad. I always thought I could handle this first year of law school. But things changed today. I just got home from my first exam. I am spent, and I am scared, and I think I failed, and I have four exams left. Talk about the long road ahead. I can barely find my way off of the front porch. I wasn't quite sure where the challenge was in my first year of law school, but at this moment I feel like I am caught in a B-list horror film, about to open the door that everyone in the audience knows should not be opened. I am lost and know no other way out. I have to open the door and face the monster that will inevitably start a string of events that may end in my ultimate demise. Exams are scary and I am scared. The first year of law school is frighteningly challenging. What was once a fairy tale has now turned into a nightmare. Just like a horror film where the predictable victims start the movie with such hope, such dreams, such plans; only to be crushed by a three-foot doll with a knife or a psycho with poor manners and even worse taste in clothing. I began this year with such high expectations and now I have hit rock bottom. Is there any way out or am I stuck in this nightmare until I fail out of law school. Well, it has been a fun ride.

Just Another Four-Letter Word

E-X-A-M. I am sure if we apply ourselves for a few seconds, we can all think of far worse four letter words. Just think about what you yell when you are cut off on your way to school or when you find out your loan is going to be late. Very rarely do we actually yell out the word exam at the top of our lungs to demonstrate our anger and frustration. So what is so intimidating about the word exam? Law students consider exam to be the worst four-letter word you will ever hear or say during your first year.

But let's take a second and be optimistic and realistic and think of a few more four-letter words: P-A-S-S; O-V-E-R; W-E-L-L; as in, you passed your first-year exams, your first year is over, and you did well. You will pass, you will do well, and it will eventually be over, no matter how far away that last exam may seem. Hindsight will prove that it wasn't that bad and you did just fine under the circumstances. Simply put, you can succeed.

While this chapter will present meticulous details and numerous concepts and steps, do not be overwhelmed by what may seem to be an endless amount of work and guidance. Attention to detail and proper preparation are the underlying tones of this chapter. Mix in some helpful hints and a good bit of hard work, and you will be able to handle your first-year exams. If you follow the steps in this chapter, you will not only pass your exams, but they will become a distant memory after you have completed law school and have started your law career. So take this chapter in stride and focus on the advice presented. I did not write this chapter to scare you, but rather to help you succeed and put your first-year exams in perspective.

Relax

There is no reason to feel how I felt after my first exam. I was uneducated, inexperienced, and did not know exactly what to expect or how to react to my first exam. In hindsight, all my worry and preoccupation were unnecessary and counterproductive. Thankfully they had no effect on the rest of my tests, as my grades increased as the exam period progressed. I learned quickly what to expect and how to react to the overwhelming tests. It is almost laughable when I read the journal entry at the start of this chapter, because it was such an unrealistic and unhealthy response to my first exam. This chapter will cover every aspect of exams, from simple preparation to exam-taking techniques and everything in between, so when you enter your exams you will be prepared, and when you exit your exams you will be able to focus on the next monster and not on your previous battle.

(IN)sider's Guide

Attorney Advice

Attorney Jessica Gordon says, "In your first year your job is to be a law student and to learn the basics of the law. You may decide to join a club or two, or to work part-time, but the vast majority of your time should be spent studying. This is a foundation year, and your grades this year will follow you throughout your career. The grades you receive in your first year will help to determine your first summer employment, which is key to your employment during your second summer, which usually is followed by a permanent offer. Your grades also affect whether or not you will make law review, which is important for developing your legal research and writing skills and is important to your future employers. If ever there was a time to put all of your energy into your studies, your first-year exams is the time, and you will appreciate that effort later on."

The most important thing to remember is to focus on the "controllables." You cannot control your exam schedule and you certainly cannot control how tough the exam actually is. However, you can control your preparation and your attention to studying. Your first-year grades are based on your first-year exams. More times than not your first year will be a great measuring stick as to your overall performance in law school. Do not underestimate the power of studying and the value of succeeding on your first-year exams. However, put this in perspective and remember that you have the answers and you have the ability—you just have to combine your abilities with diligence and proper preparation.

INsider's Guide

Attorney Advice
Attorney Sarah Kass says, "My greatest challenge in law school was trying not to get discouraged after I got my first-semester grades. Everyone in law school is used to getting As. But, of course, very few people get those grades in law school. I overcame this just by talking to professors and other classmates. I also adjusted my study habits after my first year and found a method that worked better for me, which resulted in significantly higher grades."

Take your first-year exams and grades very seriously, as they will affect the rest of your law school journey. However, keep them in perspective and know that there is a learning curve to the entire process. It is inevitable that you will be challenged more than you ever have before, and you may get lower grades than those you are used to. But you are not alone, and once you learn the ropes you will have a greater chance to succeed earlier on. This chapter was written to give you the tools you need to succeed.

Monsters under the Bed
Almost all your grades in your first year of law school classes will be based on one examination at the end of the semester. If your course is year-long, then each exam will account for one-half of your final grade, with the professor averaging the two together to reach a final number. Needless to say the sheer idea of one three-hour performance accounting for your entire semester's grade is quite stressful. It is normal to be anxious, nervous, and a little afraid. However, these emotions should only motivate you to work harder and focus longer.

At times, professors will base your final grades on other aspects such as class participation, papers, or group projects. Regardless, your first-year grades will be based predominately on your first-year exams. That being said, let's focus on the three different types of exams you may see during your first year.

Closed-Book, Closed-Note, in-Class Exams

The test: Closed-book, closed-note, in-class exams are by far the most used type of tests during your first year. More often than not every one of your first-year courses will be tested through an in-class, closed-note test. This test will usually consist of a large fact pattern and subsequent questions that you will have to answer. These questions will test various issues presented in the fact pattern. Sometimes you will be faced with multiple choice questions or even short answer, but first-year course professors usually focus their time and effort on closed-book exams consisting of one or two large fact patterns.

The challenge: The challenge with a closed-book, in-class exam is twofold. The first part of the challenge is working within the time constraints, as most professors will only allow students one exam period to complete this work (generally a three-hour session). The second part of the challenge is issue spotting and applying the law. Because of the sheer size of the fact pattern (I had an eight-page fact pattern my first year), you will have to read through a large amount of information and hone in on the most important and relevant pieces of information to discuss in your answer. In addition to spotting issues in the fact pattern, you will be faced with the challenge of applying the black letter law to these issues. Proper studying will prepare you with knowledge of the law and the ability to quickly and efficiently discuss the various caveats and issues.

Open-Book, Open-Note, in-Class Exams

The test: Open-book, open-note, in-class exams are essentially the same as closed-book exams except that you have all available resources in your hands. The answers are literally in front of you. Some professors may narrow your resources by only allowing you to bring in those resources and notes that you prepared on your own, while other professors will allow you the comfort of bringing in any hornbook, study guide, or outline that you can get your hands on. Many times professors will make these types of tests far more specific given that you can refer to your books and notes during the actual test.

The challenge: The challenges with open-book, open-note exams are far different from the challenges created by closed-book exams. Here, too, your biggest challenge is twofold. First, you do not want to rely too heavily on your notes and textbook, because you simply will not have the appropriate time to scour these resources for the answer. Your notes should never be used as a crutch or a substitute for preparation and studying, as doing so will hurt your test performance and grades. Secondly, open-book tests allow professors to hammer in the details. Thus, preparing those resources you plan on bringing into the exam will be a challenge during your studying period. Highlighting and tagging those subjects and details your professor drilled into your head during class will help with the details you will face on the exam.

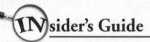

IN sider's Guide

Attorney Advice

Attorney Sara Barker says, "Open-book exams can be tricky, but they also allow you to take a different approach when preparing for them. On open-book exams where I could anticipate questions, I wrote out a sample answer and brought it into the exam and just filled in the blanks with the specific facts and my analysis. For example, in civil procedure, I wrote out my approach to a personal jurisdiction question; and in torts, I wrote out my approach to a negligence question. This way, I didn't waste time during the exam worrying about how to word definitions and how to structure my answers."

Take-Home Exams

The test: Take-home exams are a wild card of sorts. You never really know what to expect, because pretty much everything is fair game in one form or another. Professors give two types of take-home exams. The first type is where professors give students a specific time period to complete the exam outside of class. Many times this period will be twenty-four hours, requiring students to prepare for the exam before they take it but allowing them to use all available resources at the same time. The second set of circumstances is when professors allow students to use the entire exam period (which consists of all the time between the date exams begin and the date exams end on your school's calendar) to finish a take-home exam which will allow you to focus your efforts on the questions at hand and have no time constraints when taking the actual exam.

The challenge: The challenge with take-home exams can come from many different angles. First and foremost, the sheer size of the exam can be overwhelming and extremely time-consuming. I once had a take-home exam that I had twenty-four hours to complete and wrote close to forty-five pages to answer the questions. This is an amazing amount of information to discuss, and while I did it in the comfort of my own home, there was nothing comfortable about taking such a challenging test. Another challenge comes in the form of the inevitable rain cloud. When you take an exam in class, you spend three hours on the exam and move on. Take-home exams follow you around like a little rain cloud hanging over your head because you can always write more and work on the exam longer. Finally, take-home exams can be very detail oriented and call for a monumental amount of research and additional work to complete. While you may not have time limits and will not feel rushed, take-home exams can be as stressful, if not moreso, than in-class exams.

There is little, if any, predictability as to the types of exams you will see during your first year of law school. It depends almost entirely on the professors' preferences and your school's policies. Do not concern yourself too much with worrying over such trivial matters, because you will find out on the first day of class exactly what the course calls for and what type of exams you will have to take. You can also easily refer to your school's Web site before classes begin and oftentimes syllabi will be posted for your courses. Refer to the exam portion of your syllabus and you will be able to find out exactly how you will be tested on the material.

Scheduling and Exam Prep

Once you know exactly how you will be tested, it is time to start preparing for your test. Exam preparation is an intense and lengthy process that calls for diligence and attention to detail. Because of the large amount of information you will deal with during your first year, it is extremely vital to your success to start preparing early. This process begins with scheduling your semester in an organized and efficient manner so that you can complete your objectives and stay on course during the long road ahead.

The best way to start scheduling your semester to alleviate the strain of exams is to sit down in front of a calendar the first week and take out each of your syllabi. Mark down your exam dates and reading assignments for each class. Furthermore, if any of your courses have other assignments such as papers or memos, note those dates in your calendar as well so you have a visual image of your responsibilities. Once you can visualize your responsibilities, you can truly tackle them. Use different colored pens for each course and make sure your calendar is correct and organized.

When scheduling, take into account the time you will allot each week for outlining. I always found it useful to outline on a biweekly basis in order to stay on top of the material while it was still fresh in my head and to make sure that when finals came along, I was not playing catch-up with the material. Outlining every other week will give you enough material to spend meaningful time on without overwhelming your workload when the exam period begins, as the last thing you want to do is fall behind in your exam preparation.

While outlining and preparing for your first-year exams, do not forget that law school presents a new challenge that is unlike anything you have previously experienced. Law school exams are far different from those you took during your undergraduate years and call for far different preparation. There is significantly less wiggle room for law students, and cramming will not lead to success during your first-year exams. Focus on the material early and often and do not wait until the last minute to start your exam prep.

(IN)sider's Guide

Attorney Advice

Attorney Ronnie Victor says, "Do not wait until the end of the semester to do any work. It is extremely important that you not only stay on top of your work, but also that you start preparing for exams early, as falling behind in class can become very overwhelming and it is hard to get back on track once you are behind. Also, if you wait too long to study, what usually happens is that you only make an outline for a class and do not have time to do any application of the law (through hypos or practice exams) or that you do not have time to make an outline and use another person's outline. This is probably the best advice, yet it is the hardest to follow, especially for students who were able to 'cram' for exams in college and do well. Law school is completely different. You will not be able to cram the night before an exam and do well without prior preparation. You will do better on exams and have a lot less stress during exam time if you start preparing for exams earlier."

Outlining: An Introduction

Preparing for your exams will be one of the toughest parts of your first-year experience. Once your schedule is in place and you are temporally organized, it is time to start tackling the information that will appear on your exams. This is done through effective and efficient outlining. Outlining is far and away the most important part of your first year of law school, because your final grades will be based on your study habits and outline habits. Creating useful outlines will greatly enhance your ability to succeed. Condensing six months of information may seem overwhelming at first, but your performance while you are preparing for your exam is as important as your performance while taking the exam.

sider's Guide

Attorney Advice

Attorney Jessica Gordon says, "Start outlining as early as possible. Do not leave it to the last minute. Learn what an outline is and how you can start early on. If you leave it until the last minute, you will be concentrating too hard on getting your outline done, instead of learning what is in the outline. The reason to make an outline is so you can go through the process of learning the subject and paring it down to its essential elements as key reminders when you are taking the exam. If you do not do the preparation yourself, however, you will lose the important details that you would have learned through the process of outlining."

Outlining is the lifeline of law school. Your success in your first year will be a product of your outlining. Outlining begins from day one and continues throughout the entire semester. Thus, the most important rule when it comes to outlining is to start early. Creating a schedule will not only keep you organized, but it will also allow you to better focus your outlining skills and stay ahead of the game. If you wait until the end of the semester to start outlining, you will be playing an insurmountable game of catch-up when you should be studying for the exam and doing practice questions, as opposed to compiling raw material into a concise outline.

In addition to avoiding procrastination when it comes to your outlining, do not underestimate the value of creating your own, independent outline. The process of outlining leads directly to the process of learning the material for the specific course. Organizing, rewriting, and rethinking hard concepts are extremely effective tools in reviewing the material and reducing an overwhelming amount of information to a manageable and useful resource.

Insider's Guide

Attorney Advice

Attorney Ronnie Victor says, "A misconception among law students is that having the best outline will help you do well. Many students think that if they are given another student's outline (a previous student or from a friend) they will be able to do well. This is incorrect. The secret to outlines is in the formulation of the outline. The time, thought, and work used to create the outline are what will help you do well. As a professor of mine once said, 'You should not be secretive with your outline. Actually, the best thing you can do is to give everyone your outline, because if they are only using the one you gave them, then they are not formulating their own.'"

The message is clear. No matter who you talk to you, whether it is a current student, a successful attorney, or a professor, they will tell you the same exact thing. Successful performance on your first-year exams is based on successful outlining and preparation. And this outlining and preparation comes from your hand and your computer, not from the efforts of others. As a former first-year student, I know how intimidating preparing your own outlines can actually be. I remember sitting in front of my computer during the first few weeks of the semester with my textbook on one side and my notes on the other and thinking to myself, how am I going to formulate a working and useful outline to use on my first-year exams? Not only was I overwhelmed, but I was also lost—I could hardly even find a good place to begin. My hope with this chapter is that my confusion will be your salvation. There is no need to worry or experience unnecessary anxiety and fear, because there are specific steps you can take from the beginning of the semester to decrease your workload, increase your success, and alleviate many of the headaches most first-year students have during exam preparation.

Professor Pointer

Professor Patrick Wiseman says, "Just as you should write your own case briefs, so should you write your own outline, the point of doing an outline being to internalize the law. Relying on others' outlines will not serve the same purpose. Commercial outlines are available, of course, and there are probably student-prepared outlines floating around your school. Rely on them at your peril; if you find them of some use in helping you to prepare your own outline, then by all means use them, but there is no substitute for preparing your own outline."

Outlining in Study Groups

The first step to creating a successful outline is choosing writing partners. There is no steadfast equation for successful outlining, but many first-year students find it particularly helpful to work closely with other students to create outlines and prepare for exams. The old cliché "two heads are better than one" comes to life with your first-year outlines. Working with other students can alleviate a lot of the strain that first-year outlining creates.

While I found study groups to be very beneficial, not everyone learns the same. As illustrated above, some students may find study groups to be burdensome and distracting. No matter what advice you receive during your law school experiences, always remember who you are and what works best for you. If you are an independent learner and generally do not learn well in groups, then study groups may not be for you. However, if you find that discussion about complicated topics aids in your understanding of them, then study groups may be an appropriate study method. Whatever the case, listening to the point of view of others and discussing potential exam topics will certainly be valuable during your first-year exam prep.

Splitting up the course work defeats the purpose of creating an outline. The usefulness of an outline is not only in the end product, but also the means of obtaining it. First-year courses are like LEGOs. Each concept builds on the concept before it and in the end you have an immense house relying upon each piece for its support. Take one piece away and the house may fall, just like taking one concept out of your realm of understanding may create a ripple effect and destroy your ability to understand forthcoming concepts. Thus, focus on each concept individually and as a study group to ensure you understand everything, not just your part of the group outline.

Insider's Guide

Student Counsel

3L Tom Devine says, "Think hard about whether you want to join a study group before you actually do it. While some students find study groups to be very helpful, others can't run away fast enough from them. I always found study groups to be distracting, giving me just one more reason to chat and procrastinate. However, many of my classmates felt study groups were the reason why they succeeded during their first year."

Hints on Choosing a Study Group and Creating an Outline

Power in numbers. When it comes down to it, you know yourself best and you know what is best for your study habits. Some people work well in large groups, while others find that small groups of two or three work better. During my first year, I found it valuable to have three people in my study group so as to get multiple opinions and viewpoints, but not be overwhelmed or distracted by side chats. Furthermore, scheduling is always an issue and the more people in a group, the more schedules, egos, and attitudes you have to juggle.

Choose your groups wisely. Remember that you will be spending a lot of time with your study group preparing outlines for your courses. Thus, finding students you are compatible with is the most important part of the equation. You have to have a working relationship with your study group in order to create quality outlines. Keep your eyes open for those students who participate in class, come prepared, and show up. The last thing you want to do is carry the weight of an underprepared classmate because you made a poor choice when choosing your study groups. Do not be shy and when you meet people you find to be intelligent and well prepared, invite them to be in a study group and work on outlines together.

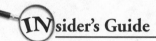

Insider's Guide

Professor Pointer

Professor Patrick Wiseman says, "Work with a study group, certainly, but do not divide responsibility for the course outline; that division of labor, while it might seem to save time, defeats the purpose of doing an outline. As the semester progresses, prepare a preliminary outline of each block of material as you move to the next. Then, as the end of the semester approaches, you will have most of the material for your outline already prepared. Do not postpone preparation of your outline to the last few weeks of the semester. By then, the task will seem daunting and will indeed be impossible to do well."

Stay on schedule. Make sure you stay on schedule. Once you form your study group, sit down with your group and set a definitive and realistic schedule that you will be able to follow, whether it be weekly, biweekly, or monthly. Make sure you are setting realistic goals as well. As each week of your first semester passes, you will have assignments to complete and outline during your review sessions. These assignments add up quickly, so stay on top of them to alleviate needless headaches and problems in the weeks before exams.

Carry your weight. Always remember that you are part of a group and the other members rely on you in the same manner that you rely on them to be available, work hard, and produce a quality outline. Make sure you prepare for class and prepare for your study group meetings so you are an active participant and not just riding your classmates' coattails. These study groups have the potential to last throughout your entire stint in law school, so make a good first impression and carry your weight to ensure the group will want to keep you as a member.

Don't overdo it. Know your limitations and stay within them. When you schedule your meetings, make sure you can attend them. Do not try to overstudy and cover an endless amount of information in each session. The quality of your work will be greatly affected and your outlines will suffer. I found the easiest way to outline was to cover a few subjects each week with my group for three hours. We found that after three hours our work went substantially south. You and your group may work longer or shorter, but the most important thing to remember is to set realistic goals for yourself and your study group.

Textbooks, Notes, and Study Guides, Oh My!

All right, your study group is in place and it is time to start outlining. The first step in outlining is choosing the resources that you will use during the outlining process. When it comes down to it, your resources can be boiled down to three distinct categories: course textbooks, class notes, and study guides (including commercial outlines, hypo-based books, and student-made outlines).

Use the following concise outline and advice when deciding exactly what the best resources are for you during the outline process:

Textbooks

What's the down-low? All of the material you cover during your first-year courses will be based on a single textbook assigned to you at the beginning of the semester. While there may be other supplements required for the course, your textbook will contain the majority of your reading and assignments. Essentially, every answer to your first-year exams can be found in your textbook. While that is somewhat comforting, the challenge comes in taking this endless amount of material and outlining it into a useful and effective document that will help you learn the law and eventually apply it on the exam.

Where's the advantage? The advantage to using your textbook during your outlining process is that all the information you need to complete your outline is at your fingertips and in one place. Furthermore, your textbook provides you with a skeleton and a flow chart for your outline. Each chapter leads to a roman numeral in your outline, so you can easily follow the ordering of your textbook during the outlining process.

Are there any disadvantages? As with all of your resources, there are disadvantages to textbooks. For starters, there is an incomprehensible amount of information in those books. By briefing your cases on a regular basis, you will have a much more concise and outlined version of the cases in the textbook, which will save you a lot of time when you begin outlining. Furthermore, sometimes textbooks do not cover the concepts of the law, but rather focus on examples of the concepts in action. Each case illustrates a concept and brings to life a real-world example of an important idea. It is your responsibility to understand this idea based on the example given in the book. Textbooks can be unclear at times and do not provide easy summaries of information, but rather call for endless reading and rereading to understand concepts that may not be nearly as difficult when phrased more directly.

Class Notes

What's the down-low? Class notes are a direct product of your efforts. In addition to your case briefs, you will be responsible for concepts and ideas presented in class that may span further than the depths of your textbook. The professor teaches according to the textbook, but she also infuses her own style and opinion as to the legal effects and nature of certain ideas. Thus, taking quality notes and paying attention in class will provide you with another resource when it is time to begin outlining.

Where's the advantage? The advantage to taking notes during class will be more than obvious when outlining. Class notes are a valuable resource, as they demonstrate the amount of time and effort you need to put into each course concept. If your first-year torts teacher spent three weeks on intentional torts and three minutes on damages, your class notes should reflect this distinction and your outline should follow accordingly. Class notes are not only great measurements of potential exam topics based on your professor's attention to specific topics, but they are also a great resource to fill in your questions and understanding of the textbook material.

Are there any disadvantages? As with any resource, there are specific concerns you should be aware of when using your class notes. Class notes should simply be used to fill in concepts and further aid in your understanding of the textbook and your case briefs. To understand your notes, you must first have read the material, so using notes you take, or those your classmates have taken, can be a crutch rather than a useful resource to reference when you have questions about the material in your textbook.

Study Guides
What's the down-low? Study guides, hypo-based books, and commercial outlines can be both helpful and harmful. If used correctly, these books can supplement your learning and reaffirm your understanding of the material. However, these should never be used as a substitute for creating your own outlines and working through the material on your own. In your first year of law school, I believe that the more resources the better, to a certain point. You do not want to overwhelm yourself with resources. Frankly, many of these materials will say the same thing but in a different way. If you understand a concept, focus on examples and hypotheticals to reinforce your understanding, as reading too much material on one concept can sometimes lead to confusion. Besides, at an average of $30 a pop, study guides can put a serious dent in your bank account. When considering study guides, always remember that you know yourself best. Use your common sense; whatever fits for you is best for you. I am only providing guidance and advice from students that came before you, but at the same time they are different from you. If you find study guides are extremely helpful, put a little more time into them. And always remember the most

important rule of study guides: If your professor wrote one, then buy it, learn it, love it, and use it.

Where's the advantage? The greatest advantage of study guides is the perspectives they present. As a first-year student, I did not find commercial outlines to be overly helpful, but I did find great value in using E & E books (examples and explanations). These types of books take particular concepts with which you will be faced and give you numerous hypos and explanations to not only reinforce the underlying ideas, but also to illustrate the caveats, exceptions, and tricks to each rule of law. Furthermore, these types of books will provide you with the best illustration of how your course topics will be tested. They give you a long, detailed hypothetical (usually mixed in with a trick or two), and ask you questions about this particular hypothetical. Going through this exercise not only reinforces concepts, but teaches you how to tackle a subject on your upcoming exam.

INsider's Guide

Attorney Advice

Attorney Sarah Kass says, "If I could attend law school again, I would use more legal supplements my first year. Since my brain was not in legal mode yet, I definitely could have used the extra help to get a more thorough understanding of the material. I also would talk to the 2Ls and 3Ls at my school about the professors and their testing styles to get a better idea of what to expect on exam day."

Are there any disadvantages? Study guides are wonderful when used properly, but can be detrimental if used as a substitute for proper preparation. Instead of making you stronger, they become a crutch. I cannot stress enough the importance of preparing your own outlines. If you feel uncomfortable or unconfident doing so, then use commercial outlines or the outlines of older students as examples instead of replacements. Commercial outlines are often too detailed and lose sight of the bigger picture. Your professors teach from a textbook, not from a commercial outline. Base your outlines on your textbook and always be a tad wary of commercial outlines and what they have to offer, because rarely are they on par with your course and your professor.

Outlining: From Beginning to End

After reading the previous sections, you should feel pretty comfortable about beginning to outline and studying for exams. Essentially the best way to look at your semester is in two parts: preparation and studying. When it comes down to it, they both present their own set of obstacles and you will spend a great amount of time on each piece of the puzzle, but preparing for studying is the far more systematic and mathematical piece of the equation. That being said, this section will focus on creating your outlines and preparing to study.

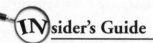

sider's Guide

Attorney Advice

Attorney Sarah Kass says, "Don't think that studying and exams in law school are anything like what you have seen in your undergraduate work. Law school is an entirely different animal and must be approached in a different way. Start early in the semester with outlines and don't be afraid to ask professors for clarification if you don't understand something. At the same time, don't get caught up in what your classmates are doing. Everyone studies and prepares differently, so figure out what works best for you and stick with it."

First things first. You are calm, collected, and have a great study group to traverse the path of your first-year exams. You feel good, confident, and are ready to get going. You and your group meet at your place and you sit down and start . . . talking about what you did last night. Wait a second. One of the hardest parts of law

ol is the newness of the situation. You probably have never
ined for exams, and if you did, it is nothing like outlining for
school. So while studying for exams may be hard enough, preparing an outline to study from seems impossible. My father used
to tell me, "Justin, the only difference between the impossible and
possible is the impossible just takes a little bit longer." And the
impossible will take a little longer. Everything seems impossible in
law school at first, but after preparation, thought, and hard work,
everything is manageable.

How to Create the Perfect Outline for Final Exams

Outline your textbook. Outlining is an overwhelming process.
You are faced with the task of reducing six months of information
and knowledge into a thirty-page tool that will end up bent, coffee
stained, triple stapled, and folded in ways you never thought paper
could fold. So the first question is, Where do I start? It seems the
most logical place to start is from the beginning of your textbook.
I found it very helpful to sit down with my textbook in hand and
use the table of contents as a skeleton for my outline. The table of
contents will provide you with a great flow chart of the information your professor will cover. Thus, take each chapter as a roman
numeral and fill in the chapter with cases and concepts as you
come across them in your outlining.

Use your case briefs. Once you have the skeleton of your outline
on paper, the next step is to start filling in each Roman numeral.
Each case in the textbook will illustrate a different part of the law.
These illustrations will be real-world examples. Include each case
in your outline along with a small section for facts and a small section for the rule from the case. This will give you a succinct summary of the material you covered in class. The best way to do this is
to refer to the case briefs that you created for class each day. If you
brief your reading each night, you will have an entirely different
and less time-consuming outlining experience than a student who
did not case brief. Once you insert all the cases in the chapter, you
are ready to move on to the next step.

Insert the case notes. After inserting your case briefs, you are ready
to review the notes after the cases in your textbook for other exam-

ples and concepts vital to your understanding of the law. After each case, the authors of the textbook insert various notes and case summaries to reinforce the black letter law presented in the lead case. Most professors assign this as part of the reading and therefore it is fair game. Make sure you review these notes and do not overlook them, as many exam questions come from this part of the reading so that students will not skip over important text. Professors will generally review the cases and then the case notes so as to pinpoint areas of interest and areas of concern for exam purposes. Take meticulous notes and highlight the material so when it is time to outline, you will be ready to roll.

Insert your class notes. Professors will spend most of the time in class reviewing cases in the textbook and teaching you the underlying concepts discussed in the actual cases. This will give you a valuable opportunity to add to your case briefs and take notes to aid in your understanding of the course material. These class notes are extremely useful when preparing your outlines. Not only do they highlight the most important parts of the textbook, but they also reinforce the legal concepts the cases discuss. After you have used your case briefs in your outline, review your class notes that cover those particular cases you are outlining and review your professor's comments on the cases. Professors practice how they play, meaning that more often than not topics they discuss thoroughly during class will often pop up on the exams at the end of the semester. Using your notes during the outline process will help you better predict the topics covered on the forthcoming exam.

Insert study guide notes. Finally, after you have inserted your case briefs and class notes, take a moment and look through each section of your outline to eliminate any cloudy areas. If for some reason you are lost or confused on a particular topic in your outline, refer to commercial study guides to better explain a complicated topic. If you are thorough when briefing, taking notes, and outlining, then you probably will need little, if any, help from commercial study guides. However, these can be great references when you find yourself stuck in a place from which you cannot find your way out. The best place to start is to find the corresponding section of the study guide that discusses your point of interest and read through it. Oftentimes these outlines will be very straightforward at first and then dive into a more detailed explanation of a particular concept. Find your area of confusion and if the commercial outline clarifies the issue, then insert the text into your outline and move on with a better understanding of the information.

Reference. While this point comes at the end of this section, referencing is something you should incorporate in your outline from the beginning of the process. Whenever you insert a case in your outline or discuss a legal concept, include the page number where you can find this information in your text. Furthermore, if you insert text from a commercial outline, do the same. This is important because you never know when you will not understand your explanation of the concept or the case, or will just want to do a little extra reading on a particular topic. The worst thing you can do while studying for exams is waste time looking for a particular case in your textbook when a few seconds during the actual outlining process will give you a specific reference as to where the text can be found. More importantly, when you are taking an open-book exam time is even more valuable, so the last thing you want to be doing during an exam is looking through your textbook because your outline is missing a reference and you need to quote a particular case.

Time-Saving Tips and Hints

All right, enough of the serious talk; let's get to some of the more exciting parts of exam taking (although they are few and far between). Exams are very straightforward. They call for preparation and studying. There is no substitute for these two pieces of the puzzle. In fact, your puzzle will be an eyesore if you try to remove either one of these two pieces from it. Exams are no different from any other part of the law school process, in that there are time savers and helpful tools you can use to make the process easier. There are no shortcuts in law school, but there are plenty of gems that will save you considerable time and effort. However, you have to know where to look, as these are not always as obvious as first-year students would like them to be. Here are some helpful hints to save time when outlining:

Use old outlines. A good place to start when outlining in order to save valuable time is to use the outlines of older students who took your course from the same professor. Rarely do professors change their teaching styles or textbooks. Generally speaking, professors use an updated edition of the same textbook and teach concepts in the same manner. This redundancy can easily work to your advantage. Talk to older students and ask if them if they have any old outlines lying around. Not only will they say yes, but they will be happy to help a struggling 1L with his or her hands out, as they were in your shoes just a few months ago. Furthermore, using older outlines will save you time with the procedural parts of the outline. Spending less time creating a skeleton for your outline or referencing your textbook for page numbers will allow you more time to focus on the substance of the outline: the law. Using older outlines will also provide you with a safety net and a resource to check your finished outlines against to ensure you outlined the course correctly.

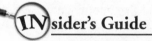

INsider's Guide

Attorney Advice

Attorney Sara Barker says, "It is very important to meet upperclassmen who had your professors and ask them for tips on how to do well in the particular class and to ask them for outlines. Once you get outlines from them, you can use these to make your own outline, and you can read the corresponding part of outline before class each day to prepare and to anticipate the kinds of issues the professor will address in class. Furthermore, while the process of making your own outline is often helpful, another suggestion that is more time effective is to take an upperclassman's outline and use it for organization and then edit it considerably by supplementing it with your notes and case briefs. The learning process is essentially the same and it can save you some serious time in the long run."

Use study guides. Using study guides can be detrimental if they are employed as a replacement for studying, but they can save serious time if they are used to clarify topics and gain thoughtful insight into cases. Sometimes you may have trouble finding a concise rule from the case, but after reading through a commercial outline, it hits you like a stack of bricks. I firmly believe your resources in law school are your best tools, but they should be used as just that: resources and not replacements. Read first, case brief second, outline third, and then refer to study guides if you are still lost. Sometimes it just takes seeing things in a different light to clarify a confusing concept, and there is no need to spend hours on something that could be solved in just a few minutes of study "guide-ance."

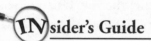 **sider's Guide**

Attorney Advice

Attorney Neera Makwana says, "Throughout the semester, always try to pay attention to what the professor is looking for in an exam answer. You can find this information by looking at old exams, paying attention throughout the semester, and talking to former students and/or the professor himself. Every time the professor mentions the exam in class, highlight and star the information provided so you can refer to it at the end of the semester. Most professors drop hints about the exam throughout the semester."

Listen to your professors. This may be not only the easiest tool to use to save time and increase your chances of success, but also the most powerful. Your professors are not trying to trick you or hide the ball when it comes down to it. In fact, they do quite the opposite. They drop subtle hints and useful guidance when it comes to your first-year exams. Your professors are predictable and it is easy to forecast the weather on exam day. This process starts by reading the syllabi for your courses. Syllabi will generally outline the form of the final exam and this will allow you to study accordingly. If the exam is multiple choice, you probably need to focus on details, whereas if the exam is essay-based, knowledge of the general concepts of law will be a good place to start. Many professors will also reward students who attend class by giving them some nuggets of wisdom when preparing for the exam. They may say a certain topic will appear on the exam or that students don't need to know much about a certain concept. Knowledge about what you don't need to focus on is as valuable as knowing what you should focus on, as it saves time and effort. Don't underestimate your professors' desire to help you pass your exams, and listen carefully when they speak, because they may just hand you a few answers if you're lucky.

DECEMBER 5, 2003

Sweat It Out

Two hours left. I have been struggling through a terrible flu and can hardly see straight. Last night was a roller coaster of getting up to re-hydrate or blow my nose and crashing back into bed. I did not sleep for more than an hour straight. On top of all that, I am convinced my dog somehow caught the flu from me because he has to use the restroom every fifteen minutes. I have forgotten what it feels like to be rested. And now I am sitting in the exam and fighting to stay awake and not explode from the pressure my sinuses are causing. "Two more hours" I repeat over and over again in my head. And then I can pass out and let this terrible case of karma (whatever did I do?!) pass. While I sit in my seat trying to remain focused and stay the course, all I can think about is how happy I am that I am prepared for this exam. If I do not succeed, at least I can blame it on the flu and not my preparation. Even though I truly believe there are two tons of mucus between my head and my hand, somehow this information is second nature to me and I don't even have to think about it. Preparation overcomes everything, even the worst flu I have ever had.

Study Time

Now that you have created an outline that even your professors would be jealous of, it is time to start studying and preparing for your exams. This is usually done in the last month building up to the actual exam. Start earlier and you will probably forget most of the concepts you learned, but start later and you will run out of time. You have completed the first part of the equation: outlining. Now it is time to focus on the second, less systematic piece of the puzzle. While studying for exams may be redundant and time-consuming, it is extremely necessary. You spent hours upon hours preparing an outline and condensing the course into manageable concepts, and now it is time to put those concepts into your head and make them your second nature.

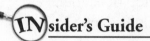

IN sider's Guide

Attorney Advice

Attorney Rena Seidler says, "When it comes to studying try different things. Don't limit yourself during your first semester to always studying alone, or with a study group, or using a certain type of study aid. Trying a variety of study techniques enables you to better find out what works for you. And if you can't think of an effective way to study, ask your professors. They are experts on law school and studying, and talking with them helps you establish a good rapport that may benefit you later on in school or in your career."

Tips to Get You Prepared for the Final Exam

Plan ahead. The first thing you should do when studying is plan ahead and schedule the upcoming weeks of your life. As a first-year student you will generally be faced with four to five exams during your first semester. The best policy is to start about a month to a month and a half before the exam period actually begins. Most schools allot two to three weeks for exams and stagger your tests out every four to five days to keep you on a slow-paced schedule. Enjoy this while it lasts because in the years to come you may have two exams on the same day, a daunting task even for the most pre-pared students. Most students start about a month before the exam period and tackle a subject a week. You should reverse the order of your exams and tackle the subjects in that order, studying for your last exam first and your first exam last. That allows you to spend the week and a half or so before your first exam to study solely for that exam. Once you hit the exam period, you can use the days in between exams to study for the upcoming exams. Following this schedule gives you about five to ten days to focus on each topic. If you are properly prepared and outlined, then these days can be used to do practice problems and reinforce tough concepts, along with filing that outline of yours into the center of your head.

Review your outline. I always liked to start my exam prep by thoroughly reviewing my outline for the first couple of days. This will give you a basic understanding of the material along with the opportunity to fill in holes or reinforce tough concepts. While the most important piece of the first-year exam puzzle is to under-stand concepts and feel comfortable applying them to hypotheti-cals, many times there will be concepts you have to memorize. More often than not, you will face concepts with elements (such as intentional torts) or specific rules and statutes. Memorizing these elements and rules is essential to applying the concepts in an exam setting, because if you don't know the elements, then you surely cannot work through the problem and identify a potential answer to the question. So take the first few days and familiarize yourself with your outline and the ideas that are covered in each course.

Hypothesize. The next step is to begin practice problems. You should spend most of your time doing practice problems. These can range from hypos found in study guides to old tests. The examples and explanation books are wonderful resources. They quickly explain a concept and then give multiple hypos testing that particular concept. Go through the book and take good notes on the subjects, as this will reinforce different important rules of law. When doing practice problems, make sure your outline is close to you. Hopefully, you can begin by looking at a hypo and referring to your outline to find the answer. This will familiarize you with the outline and act as a checks-and-balances system, ensuring that the answers to different types of hypos are actually in your outline.

By the time the exam is near, you should be able to answer questions without referring to your outline, because all that wonderful information will be second nature to you.

Meet with friends. One of the most important rules you can learn from this book is to use your resources. They save time and effort, and increase your likelihood of finding success in your first year. Your classmates are valuable resources in the weeks leading up to your exams. They can answer questions, clarify concepts, and work diligently with you to review topics that are hard to understand. They are in the same boat as you and want to succeed just as much as you do. Each student views the law through his or her own personal looking glass. While you may view a concept a certain way, you can never have too many perspectives and views to consider. Use your classmates' looking glasses, as they may provide you with a different unique argument, or even point out flaws in your arguments and understanding of the law, all of which are valuable resources on exam day.

Meet with your professors. Your professors are the best predictors of what will be on your exam, because they create it. Just by talking to them you will gain a better understanding as to what they are looking for on their exams and what may or may not be tested for on the exams. Furthermore, when studying for exams, if you have questions, professors are always happy to talk to you and review difficult concepts with you before the actual exam. I always found it helpful to meet with my professors about a month before each exam to ask them to review my outline. If nothing else, it will be nice to know if you are going in the right direction with your outline and your preparation. Discussing your preparation tactics and seeking advice from professors can be very helpful. I have had numerous professors point me in the direction of a study guide or a topic to focus on, and then, magically, these topics appear on the exam. Do not underestimate the value face-to-face meetings can have. Showing your professors you want to succeed opens many closed doors and may even result in a few helpful hints and resources when studying for their exam.

Use CALI and other online resources. There is an abundance of online resources available to first-year law students through their school, ranging from LexisNexis to Westlaw to CALI (the Center for Computer-Assisted Legal Instruction). Any and all of these provide students with extensive review programs for each first-year course along with a large array of practice problems and explanations. These are another great resource for you to use, as they are free and extremely helpful in explaining and testing difficult concepts that are likely to appear on your first-year exams. The best part about these is that they are as useful as study guides but do not cost anything and are available to most first-year students. CALI lessons download to your computer so you can always have them at your fingertips when traveling, or anytime you are away from your textbooks. They also mix things up a bit and provide another way to review without having to stare at a book. And with as much studying as you will be doing during your first semester, anything to break up the redundancy of staring at a book will be a welcome distraction.

Work through old exams. Furthermore, most professors will give students an opportunity to look over old exams. This is a wonderful learning tool and the best predictor as to what to expect on exam day. Going through the actual exercise of taking an exam under time constraints before you actually sit for the real exam will give you a better feel for what to expect when your performance really matters. Did you know that before police officers get their badge they are pepper sprayed? The reason why they do this is so they know what it feels like and how to react if they are actually sprayed in the line of duty. While exam taking is not nearly as painful, taking one on the chin before your actual exam illustrates the same point: You know what to expect, you understand the process, and you won't panic nearly as much. Taking practice exams also lets you hypothesize as to what you may see on your forthcoming exams. The bottom line is that there are only so many ways to test a concept and if you happen to see a common trend or question throughout a professor's practice exams, then take note because you may see a similar question on exam day.

Studying for exams can seem overwhelming at first, as you will be faced with an unbelievable amount of information to learn. However, most of this information need not be memorized. All you need to do is understand the concepts and demonstrate that you can apply them in an effective and efficient manner. Rarely will you have to memorize pages of information, so don't flip out when looking at your outline in the beginning. Hypos will demonstrate common themes and concepts tested. Learning the hypos is as important as learning the law and will make the law school world seem a whole lot more manageable. Plan early and stay the course. It is only one month of diligent studying and then you are free for your winter break. No matter how bad it seems, it will not last forever, and you will succeed if you prepare properly and study diligently with attention to the details. The small things are what make the difference between an A student and B student. Focus on those details and follow the steps we have talked about to be part of the top 10 percent in your first year. Sometimes they say that in law school you are just a number—so why the hell not be the highest number possible?

Taking an Exam

Taking an exam for the first time is stressful. It is a new experience and a challenging experience, but it does not have to be an overwhelming experience. Exams are very manageable if you know what to expect and are prepared for each subject. Professors are not trying to fail you. In fact, most professors are trying to reward students who worked hard, stayed on top of the reading and case briefing, and studied diligently for the exam. Because you will certainly fall within these categories, you will do just fine. You have been studying and reviewing for weeks now, and the exam is finally here. Studying is over at this point and it is time to start focusing on taking the actual exam. Here is a step-by-step guide as to what you should be doing in the final hours before the exam. Let's take a walk through the entire process, starting from the night before.

Relax the Night Away

You should use the night before an exam to relax, clear your mind, and focus on the next day. In a perfect world, you shouldn't study much the day before the exam. Realistically, if you don't know it by now, you aren't going to learn it in one day. This isn't undergraduate school, and cramming generally doesn't pay off. However, if you do feel you need to study the day before an exam, do so moderately and don't wear yourself out, because you need to be ready to rock the next day.

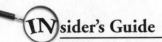sider's Guide

Professor Pointer
Professor Patrick Wiseman says, "As the dreaded moment approaches, try not to dread it. Keep things in perspective. It's likely that this first exam counts for only three credits or so, maybe some 3 percent of the credits required to graduate. I know from personal experience that first-semester grades are not necessarily a good predictor of later law school performance. Of course, in your case, they might be; I didn't have the benefit of this advice!"

By about midafternoon, put the outlines down, organize your materials for the exam, and begin relaxing. Go work out, take a long walk, watch a movie, cook some dinner, shop—whatever takes your mind off of stressful situations. It is completely normal to be anxious and a little stressed out about the next day, but don't freak out, because that will get you nowhere. Take half of the next day and the evening to rejuvenate your mind and your body. Go to sleep early and make sure you have a good meal before you call it a night. Take care of yourself physically before an exam, because the last thing you want is to walk into the classroom tired, or with a headache, or a hangover, or feeling overly anxious.

"Time" for Exams
All right, the day is finally here. You are excited, nervous, anxious, but most importantly, you are ready. Exams are generally three hours long and start in the morning, afternoon, or evening (9 A.M., 1 P.M., and 6 P.M., but it really all depends on your particular school). Each starting time carries its own set of concerns and issues. No matter what time your exam starts, you should always

plan on arriving at school at least thirty minutes ahead of time to ensure you are in your seat and ready to roll before the doors close. The last thing you want is to be late for an exam. You will still be able to take it, but you will have lost valuable time that you will almost certainly need.

Take a look at the following details of what you should be thinking about and the considerations you should take depending on the time for your exam.

Morning Exams

The beloved morning exam. Make sure you are up early enough to get dressed, take a shower, eat breakfast, and get to the exam early. Also allot a few minutes to read the newspaper or a magazine. This is a helpful tool to wake up your mind and get things going. It is sort of like warming up before the marathon. You don't want to hit the starting line cold. Consider traffic on your way to school, as you will inevitably be in the car or on a train during the morning rush.

Afternoon Exams

These exams fall right after your lunch break. Hopefully you won't have any issues getting up and getting to school, but you still may get caught in a bit of lunch hour traffic, so allot the appropriate amount of travel time. The big issue here involves food. It is important to eat before exams, but you don't want to overeat. Overeating or overdrinking can lead to frequent bathrooms breaks. Furthermore, if you eat a large meal before an exam, you might find yourself fighting to stay awake. Just think about how badly you need a nap after Thanksgiving dinner. Fulfill your appetite, but don't overdo it.

Night Exams

In my opinion these exams can often be the most challenging, because you have all day to think about them. Have a nice, relaxing day leading up to the exam so you are rejuvenated and energetic when you sit down in the classroom. Traffic will generally be at its worst during this exam period, so allot some extra time to get to school. Take a nap during the day if you feel lethargic, and make sure you have a snack to eliminate hunger issues before the exam.

Do not put too much concern into the time of your exam, as there is really nothing you can do to change it. Take the necessary precautions and steps to avoid traffic and hunger and remember that if you are prepared for your exam, you will be fine no matter what time it is.

Accessorize

When it is time to pack your bags for your exams, make sure you overpack. Imagine you are staying in a tropical storm where the weather is unpredictable. It will only last three hours, but you need to make sure you are ready for anything and everything.

ACCESSORIES TO BRING TO YOUR EXAMS

☐ **Sweater/sweatshirt/long-sleeved shirt:** Whatever it may be, just take along something to keep you warm if you are under an air conditioning vent.

☐ **Snack food:** Don't take anything with too much salt or sugar, as you don't want a headache or a sugar rush.

☐ **Beverage:** Water is the best choice, and definitely make sure your drink has a screw-on cap to prevent a spill on your laptop or exam.

☐ **Extra pens/pencils:** You will always need a writing utensil to take notes before you start writing. If the exam is multiple choice, bring in a few number-two pencils to fill in those pesky bubbles.

☐ **Highlighters:** These are great to highlight important parts of the fact pattern that you may want to discuss in your answer.

☐ **Pain Reliever:** You never know when you may get a headache. An even better approach is to take a couple of pills before your exam just to make sure a headache doesn't backdoor its way into your exam performance.

- ❏ **Scratch paper:** Just in case your school does not provide you with blue books to write in, you may want to have a few extra pieces of paper to take notes and outline your answers.
- ❏ **Outline and textbook:** If you are taking an open-book exam, you will obviously want to make sure you bring in your book, but don't forget to bring your outline as well. Do not rely on them too much, but they will be nice to have if you forget the elements of a crime or the name of an important case.
- ❏ **Earplugs:** Silence is golden. Being able to concentrate without hearing coughing, sneezing, tapping, typing, and any other distracting noise will keep you focused on the task at hand and prevent needless mind-wandering.
- ❏ **Your laptop:** I know it is silly to point this out, but if you are taking an exam on your laptop, bring it along with the necessary accessories such as a power cord, a floppy drive, or whatever else your school may require.
- ❏ **Exam schedule:** Make sure you print out your exam schedule along with a detailed list of the exam rooms and times. The last thing you want to do is arrive at school and waste valuable time looking for your exam classrooms.
- ❏ **Money:** Make sure you have a few extra bucks on you in case you need to pay for parking or get hungry or thirsty.

This is just a checklist of the most important things you should consider when packing for your exams. You know yourself best and you should pack accordingly. If you never get cold, then don't worry about a sweater, and if you are always cold, wear pants and bring a few warm items. Always refer to your syllabus before the day of your exam for specific exam instructions, because your professor's wishes (no matter what they may be) will always prevail.

The First Test

Once you are sitting in your exam room and the exam is passed out, your first task begins. The first task on any exam is reading the instructions, the fact pattern, and the questions. Each one of these tasks presents its own set of issues. When reading through the instructions, ask yourself, "What is the professor asking me to do with this exam?" This is a simple task, but an important question. Many times the instructions will tell you exactly what professors are looking for on their exams. Some professors may ask you to discuss the issue and come to a specific conclusion, while other professors may not care about the conclusion, but would rather you focus on your thought process in arriving at it. Read the instructions carefully and note exactly what the professor wants you to do on the exam.

IN sider's Guide

Student Counsel

3L Tom Devine says, "I always found it very helpful to take a rubber band into the exam with me and place it around my wrist. When I started freaking out or loosing concentration, I would pop myself once with it. Not a pain inducing, bloody wrist pop, but just hard enough to bring me back to reality and keep my mind where it needs to be, on the exam."

Once you have read the instructions, turn to the questions on the exam. I like to read the questions before the fact pattern, because when you are reading the fact pattern you can look for answers. If there are no questions about a particular issue, then you do not need to focus your reading on that particular part of the fact pattern. Never skip any pieces of the fact pattern, and read all footnotes and endnotes, because you never know when a helpful piece of information will be found in those small additions to the exam.

After reading the questions, it is time to take a look at the lengthy fact pattern. This is a great point to bust out those trusty highlighters and pens and start marking up the exam. I always like to read through the fact pattern twice. The first time, I read through the facts to gain a basic understanding of the issues. Most fact patterns are extremely detailed and walk you through a series of wildly fictionalized events that could only occur on a law school exam. After you have a basic understanding of the facts, take a moment and go back through the fact pattern, highlighting important issues, circling names and dates, and underlining specific facts you will discuss in your answer. This will ensure that you don't miss any issues and can easily refer back to the fact pattern for names and dates, saving valuable time as you are outlining your answer.

INsider's Guide

Professor Pointer

Professor Roy Sobelson says, "I wish more students would take to heart their professors' advice to outline their exam answers before writing them. Some do fine without them, but a huge number of the poor exams do not show any sign of outlining or planning. Outlining is important for at least two reasons. One is that professors are looking for issue recognition skills more than the ability to repeat black letter law. Outlining gives the student a more disciplined approach to defining and discussing each separate issue. It also reduces the amount of time spent wandering all over the place before making some critical points. Another advantage to outlining is that students are often unable to finish an exam. If a student outlines and then sets out the issue statements on the exam, she may get at least some credit for defining an issue she was unable to fully address."

Manage Your Time

This section may seem pretty obvious, but nonetheless it should be mentioned. Managing your time during the exam is one of the most challenging but effective ways to succeed. Many exams will have multiple questions and they may not be weighted evenly. The last thing you want to do is spend half of your exam period answering a question that only counts for 15 percent of the exam. While you may have a great answer and get full credit, there is still another

85 percent of the exam that you have to complete. An easy way to solve this problem and avoid over answering is to allot the appropriate time to each question. If a question counts for 50 percent of the exam, then allot 50 percent of the exam time to answer that question. I like to look through the directions (your professor will generally note the weights assigned to each question), and then quickly calculate how much time I should spend on each question and write that time next to the question. It keeps me focused and within my temporal limitations.

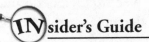 **sider's Guide**

Attorney Advice

Attorney Neera Makwana says, "Be sure to always organize your answer from the start. This way you can be sure your answer flows smoothly and you won't miss any important issues. When I was a law student, I usually wrote my whole exam answer in outline form and then went back to expand them into sentences (I took my exams by computer). That way, if for some reason I did run out of time, I had all the major issues down for some partial credit."

Outlining Exam Answers

Most students and professors find it extremely helpful to take the first third of the exam period to outline answers to the question. This allows you to organize your thoughts and answer each question thoroughly. Outlining your answers may cost you some time up front, but it will inevitably save you time toward the end of the exam—and if you run out of time, you can insert your outline into your answer so you receive partial credit for the question.

Steps to Take When Outlining an Exam

Step One: *Summarize the questions.* The first step to creating your outline is to summarize the questions your professor has asked. Insert the questions into your outline as headers if there are multiple questions. If you are only asked one question, then insert it at the top of the page and move on to the next step. Keeping the questions in front of you while working on your answer will help you stay the course and prevent unnecessary tangents. Every sentence in your answer should play a role and serve a purpose. Otherwise it is a waste of time and space.

Step Two: *Insert the facts.* After you summarize each exam question, the next step is working through the difficult and often lengthy and detailed fact pattern. Your answers will be based on the specific facts at hand. Each fact adds a piece to the puzzle and can often change the entire result. One of the most overwhelming tasks on exam day is using the facts in your favor for answering the questions. Underline important facts within the exam and insert those facts under the summarized questions in your outline. When you return to your outline to formulate your answers, you will find your task significantly less daunting, as you will have everything you need to answer the questions right in front of you.

Step Three: *Place them in order.* As you begin filing the facts away in your outline, always consider chronological events within the fact pattern. When you are dealing with issue spotting and see a variety of issues that fall under one question, make sure you insert them in the order in which they occurred, along with the corresponding date. This will allow you to not only gain a sense of how the story unfolded, but dates also generally serve a purpose on an exam. They may create issues involving statute of limitations (which is the time a party has to bring a case before they lose those rights) or even elements of a concept (such as the temporal requirements for adverse possession of property). Inserting these issues under your question heading in chronological order will help you spot issues and maintain organized thoughts as you work through your exam.

So now that you have summarized the questions and inserted the pertinent facts chronologically under those question headings so they don't get lost in the mix, it is time to take your outline and turn it into a more cohesive, logical answer. Under each section heading, insert the following headings as small letters or numbers:

I-R-A-C. Now you are ready to move on to the next step in the exam process.

IRAC

IRAC is quite possibly the most important acronym you will ever hear in law school. While I didn't invent this concept, it becomes common knowledge to law students and is a great method to use when answering a test question. IRAC is the process you follow to deal with legal issues and questions on the exam. This is the final step in the outlining process, but it is also the most difficult. Once you have your issues and facts organized under your question headings, it is now time to formulate a direct and organized response to the question.

(I): Issue

Once you have your questions properly arranged at the head of each section and the corresponding facts are in place within your outline, it is time to identify the issue under each question. The answer to each question will be based on the outcome of a specific issue, which illustrates the importance of understanding how to create a useful issue statement. The issue essentially summarizes the legal question you are addressing. This is generally a combination of the professor's question and those pertinent facts relating to the question. For example, let's say your professor asks you on the exam, "What are the damages that will be rewarded to person A if he wins his case?" and you quickly read through the exam and find the statement, "Person A's wife was killed in an automobile accident when Person B collided with Person A's wife after leaving a bar noticeably drunk." Combining the question and statement would give you the following issue statement: "The issue in this case is whether Person A can recover damages from Person B for the death of his wife even though he suffered no personal injuries nor was in the car during the accident." Since there may be multiple exam questions based on the fact pattern, you will have to repeat this process for each question asked by your professor. Issue spotting and creating issue statements takes practice, but once you can decipher an issue statement, your job for the rest of the exam will be pretty easy, as all you will need to do is address that statement in order to answer the question.

(R): Rule

The next step in the IRAC process is finding the rule of law applicable to the issue. Since the issue is essentially a statement posing a particular point of law, the rule is the answer found within the law. Once you take a minute and review your issue statement, think back to your outline and ask yourself, "What part of the law applies to this issue?" Looking to the previous issue statement, we should immediately think about the rule of law governing damages. In addition to considering the law governing damages and where and when they may be available, you should consider where this law comes from and what it suggests in relation to your issue statement. Once you find the applicable rule of law based on your outlining and case briefing, you can easily move on to the next part of the IRAC process.

(A): Apply

The next step in the IRAC process is applying the rule of law to the specific issue. Applying the rule can be challenging, but is also extremely important to your success on exams. Simply stating the rule does not illustrate your understanding of the question or the law. Applying the rule of law can be challenging because most fact patterns will create situations with multiple outcomes. There simply will not be any right or wrong answer. Rather, there will be an opportunity to discuss how the rule can be applied to the set of facts. Your success on an exam is not found in your answer, but rather the process you take to obtain your answer. It is wonderful to spot an issue and state the applicable law, but applying the rule to the facts is really your time to shine on your exam. When applying the rule of law, you should consider discussing the following:

The court's interpretation of the rule of law

The court's explanation of how the rule of law should be applied

Caveats concerning the specific rule (limitations, exceptions, and multiple applications of the rule)

Analogizing the rule of law from a case to your current fact pattern

Important policy considerations (as to why the court decided one way or another or even created the rule of law)

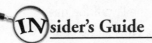

INsider's Guide

Attorney Advice

Attorney Sara Barker says, "My greatest challenge in law school was learning how to issue spot and take a law school exam, which was drastically different from any exams I had taken in college. Something helpful that I did was I wrote out answers to practice questions and discussed my approach to the questions with professors during office hours. I made sure to have an issue statement for each question on the practice exam so they could specifically comment on it, as most of your performance on an exam will be based on your ability to create a solid issue statement. Also some professors gave out sample answers to their practice exams, and I studied those and tried to mimic the style and format of their answers."

By following this process, you will essentially show your thought process and work before you come to a conclusion of law. If the rule of law you are dealing with is different from those facts presented to you on the exam, take the time to discuss why this rule is applicable to the question but justifies a different conclusion of law based on the differences between the facts you are presented with and those of the case which created the applicable rule.

Professor Pointer

Professor Patrick Wiseman says, "Do not jump to conclusions. I won't say that to every rule there is an equal and
opposite rule. But I will say that you should at least consider
the possibility that the conclusion you've reached is not the
only possible conclusion. For every declarative sentence you
write, at the very least think 'on the other hand . . .' and
think it seriously—but do not make up the law. If the rule
you're applying is universally applied, then there is no occasion for 'on the other hand,' at least as to the applicable
rule. Then again, rarely is application of a rule, even one
universally followed, so formalistically straightforward, so
you should consider the possibility that perhaps, in the circumstances of the particular case, the purpose of the rule
might be ill-served by its application."

(C): Conclusion

This leads to the final step of the IRAC process, which is coming to a conclusion based on your issue and the rule of law. The
first step when coming to a conclusion is taking a quick peek
at the instructions and finding out what the professor wants in
your conclusion. Some professors may want you to argue both
sides of the law and present a likely outcome, while other professors may call for you to persuasively argue one side and support
a steadfast and direct conclusion. Your conclusion should be a
clearly stated sentence or two summarizing your points and taking a stance. Do not spend too much time on your conclusion
because most professors are more interested in how you reached
a specific conclusion than what that conclusion may be. However, be concise and direct, saying something like, "Based on the
analysis of the rule discussed above, a court will likely decide in
favor of the plaintiff because the defendant was negligent in his
actions and a husband can require damages for that negligence

even though he suffered no direct personal harm." Your conclusion can be more detailed, but do not lose sight of the ultimate goal of a conclusion, which is summarizing your argument and taking a stance.

The IRAC process is a wonderful opportunity to use a systematic equation on your exam. It not only gives you a detailed approach to tackling a tough task, but will also allow you a checklist and a map to navigate through the exam. Practicing the IRAC process before exam day will serve you well, as the last thing you want to do is use it for the first time on your first exam. Use IRAC on practice exams so you are aware of the steps and can better manage the process and your time as you work through it. Each step of the process builds on the previous steps, so it is important to tackle every step and move forth until you have completed the entire IRAC process.

Review

Once you are done with the IRAC process, you have essentially completed your exam-day tasks. If you are one of the fortunate few to have some remaining time, read through your exam for grammar and spelling. Most professors do not deduct points for spelling or grammar, but there is no harm to demonstrating your understanding of the English language. Focus especially on legal terms, as you should be familiar with the spelling and use of those terms. Professors have to read through a large number of exams in a short period of time, so anything you can do to make it easier for them to read your exam will only be beneficial to your grades and performance. Furthermore, take a few moments and reread the exam to ensure you have answered each question posed and did not overlook any important facts presented in the lengthy fact pattern. It is one thing if you lose valuable points because you did not answer a question correctly, but don't be the student who does not get credit for an answer because you forgot to deal with the question. Remember that you will never get credit for something that you didn't write.

Attorney Advice

Attorney Nick Goldberg says, "When you are taking an exam, err on the side of putting too much info on the test. I always did and it worked out. Just know the material as well as you can and then read the question very carefully, because there is nothing worse then studying for an entire semester only to answer the wrong question, when in all actuality, you knew the answer. You only get one shot! That said, try to get the nerves out, take practice exams, and study so hard that you can honestly say, 'I did all I can do.' Lots of grades in law school are subjective, so don't get down if you screw up on a test. It happens to everyone. Just make sure you pick it up and kick some butt on the next one to make up for it."

The Aftermath

At this point, the worst of it is certainly over. Your feet are officially wet and you survived your first exam. The most important thing now is to forget about it and move on. Focus on the controllables and do not stress about the past. Law school is about moving on and putting your last obstacle behind you so you can focus on the next one.

Most students fear exams because of the potential for failure. Most law students have been a success throughout their entire academic journey leading up to law school, so even the thought of failure is frightening. However, keep things in perspective. Failure is never permanent and you can always retake a course. You will not be sent to law school purgatory because you did poorly on one exam.

Things to Remember After You Take Finals

Its only one test. Do not forget that the exam you just took was only one test. It counts for half of one-fifth of your first-year grades (assuming you have five classes and each class is a one-year course with two tests weighted equally). Thus, in a one-year course, your performance on one exam will count for about 10 percent of your first-year grades. Simply put, this test does not have enough value to stress over. It does count, but you can always save one poor performance by excelling on your other exam opportunities. During my first year, I did relatively well in my classes. However, I simply could not grasp the concepts presented in the civil procedure course. I had a great professor and worked diligently on the material, but it never clicked. I did poorly on the exam. However, I did well on my other exams and those performances brought up my overall grades for my first year. The point is that each exam only counts for a fraction of your final grades, so take that into consideration and move on with your studying. After an exam, your fate is sealed. There is nothing you can do to change your performance, so do not fret, just move on and work hard to succeed on the next one.

 **INsider's Guide**

Professor Pointer

Professor Patrick Wiseman says, "Now that your exam is over, forget about it and move on to whatever's next on your agenda. Do not engage in any 'postmortem' with other students; it will drive you nuts. And do not try to predict how you did on the exam; often exams you feel the worst about will turn out to have been your best. You have earned whatever grade you have earned, and there's nothing you can do about it now. Being in law school, you were probably a pretty good student in college or university. You are probably not accustomed to getting grades in the midrange. Get used to the idea that that may be about to change. You are competing with the smartest people you've ever been among."

Get out of town. When you have finished a law school exam, take off and talk to no one. Never talk to your classmates about an exam that you just took. This will only create unnecessary stress and headaches. Your classmates will almost inevitably ask you if you wrote this or if you answered that. They will probably have different responses to the questions and different reactions to the exam. By listening to them and their narration of their performances, you will start to doubt your own. There is no set right or wrong on a law school exam and what may work for one student may not work for another. You may have come to a completely different conclusion than your classmates, but that does not make your performance or your answer any less correct. The best thing to do is get out of the school quickly and don't toy with the temptation of discussing the exam. The best thing you can do is leave the past in the past and begin preparing for your next exam.

Chill. Depending on your exam schedule, you will generally have three to four days between exams. Thus, take the rest of the day and relax, chill out, kick back, and do nothing. Recharge your mind and refresh your body. Exams are extremely testing (no pun intended) and take a lot of energy out of you. Your mind will be shot and your body will ache. However, you have to do it four more times. The last thing you want is to burn yourself out before the exam period ends, so take a day and rejuvenate so you can get down to business and start focusing on the next great obstacle.

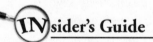

Insider's Guide

Student Counsel

3L Peter Morris says, "I always found that after an exam the best thing to do was to go to the bookstore and sell back your study guides as most bookstores buy these back. It gets them out of your face, saves you a few backaches, and puts a little cash in your pocket, my personal favorite."

Get rid of those notes. I always like to get my notes, textbooks, and study guides for a particular course out of sight once the exam is over. I do this for a few reasons. First and foremost, I do not want the temptation of looking up an answer and stressing myself out if I missed an element, an issue, or a case. Once again, the past is the past and it is time to move on. Secondly, I just can't stand to look at excessive numbers of books. Once you are done with an exam, get those books out of the way. It will not only make you feel like you accomplished something by finishing an exam (even though you are unaware of the outcome), but it will also keep you focused on the next task.

Pat yourself on the back. At this point in time, it is okay to reward yourself and pat yourself on the back. You did well. You survived your first exam. You got through a novel and challenging experience with minimal stress and anxiety. Take a moment to be proud of yourself. Pass or fail (and you will pass), you got through it, and that is more than most people can say. Be proud and crack a smile, then focus on the next one.

What a Chapter!

I know this chapter has been intense and may have even made your stomach stir a bit. But please, trust me, you will succeed and you will do fine. The great thing about law school is that it rewards hard work and dedication. If you follow this chapter and truly dedicate yourself to the process, you will not only pass, but you will be at the top of your class. That is all law school is: a process. It calls for hard work and preparation, but unlike many processes, it is almost systematic in the sense that if you follow the process, you will find success within the process. Always remember that the admissions staff at your university accepted you not only because you had the numbers and the resume, but also because they honestly thought you could succeed and master the curriculum. It is to both your advantage and theirs for you to succeed. So listen to your professors and do not take the process for granted. Professors, 2Ls, 3Ls, admissions staff, mentors, tutors, and your classmates are all there to help you pass your exams. They are the cogs that make the mechanism run. Use your resources, learn the material, practice with endless hypos and exams, and come to the exam prepared, because the process rewards those who are ready for it.

NOVEMBER 7, 2003

Twenty Words

"Twenty damn words." I said it over and over again in my head. Why can I not rid my paper of twenty damn words? Who would have ever thought that twenty words would have been the difference between a passing grade and a failing one? I never would have believed it. However, two hours before my final brief is due, I am twenty words over the page requirement and my teacher will not accept my work if I cannot shave twenty words off of my paper. I have taken out every conjunction, pronoun, adverb, and comma that I possibly can without embarrassing the entire English language. AND I AM STILL TWENTY WORDS OVER. I now have less than an hour and I am reading through a thirty-page memo and can barely tell the difference between my commas and my periods because I am so sleep deprived. I finally grab a cup of coffee, sit down in front of my laptop, and focus. I find a sentence where I used "that" unnecessarily. Nineteen words. I keep reading, skimming, and editing. I am down to two words. I finally get to the last paragraph. If it does not happen here, then it will not happen at all. I read through it twice and play grammatical survivor until I take out the two weakest links. This nightmare is finally over. I print out my paper, staple it together, and walk up the stairs to the fourth-floor secretary and hand in my finished paper. She looks at me and says, "Two minutes till it is late; you just made it." I laugh. She doesn't even know how right she is.

While I first thought that law school was established for blossoming writers with an interest in law, I was quickly proved wrong. Law school is an institution unlike any other. No prior knowledge, interests, intelligence, abilities, or skills prepare you for what you will find in this unique society. This society does not teach writing, but rather asks for writing to be a prerequisite on your resume. Therefore, as you read this chapter, you will learn the lessons that I have learned. You will find out what I found out about the first year of law school and you will understand where writing fits into the equation and what steps you can take to prepare yourself for the most challenging experience you will ever have.

The summer before my first year of law school, I kept a journal to collect my feelings and emotions, and to create a chart of my personal growth. The following entry was the first of many. I was well aware of the obstacles ahead and my greatest concern was how my writing skills would hold up against the rigorous law school curriculum.

JUNE 7, 2003

The Summer Before Law School

As I stare at my computer screen, I am well aware of the time. I know that I am rounding third and beginning the last leg of my collegiate journey before I enter the summer before law school. It almost carries a horror movie title tone, "The Summer before Law School." While I sit here, mere months away from the beginning of my future training, I meticulously think and rethink the changes I plan to make to complete my transition to my new educational path. I often wish I were a writing superhero of sorts, no weaknesses and the ability to leap tall buildings with a single bound and conquer the grammar villains. However, just as with every beginning law school student, I have my kryptonite and I have my weaknesses. As my transition begins and days pass quickly, I diligently work to improve my abstract and narrative ability, polish my grammar skills, and focus my statements to reduce the wordiness and confusion that often arises when restating similar ideas.

College Education and Law School Writing: Lessons to Learn

Throughout my educational journey in the Communication School at the University of Texas, many of my classes called for strong writing skills. Most classes asked me to write three to five papers per semester. This means I have written twenty-five to thirty papers during college. Each one of these works calls for great dedication and a desire to succeed as a writer. Rough drafts, rewrites, countless edits, attention to detail, references, citations, and thoughtful, articulated responses have become the norm in all my work because of college's expectations from its students. The writing process is truly an example of a large puzzle. Each step represents a different piece of the puzzle, and if a writer chooses to skip even one of the essential steps, the final work is incomplete, just like a puzzle with a missing piece. Therefore, by following this thorough process, I have polished many areas of my writing, from grammar rules to complicated rewrites and editing abilities.

It becomes more and more important to take the lessons you learned as a collegiate writer and apply those to any future endeavor. Law school is one such area where cultivated writing skills truly shine. Words are nothing more than the clay of the English language and only when an artist, or in this case a writer, takes this mess and shapes it into something presentable can it truly attain its power and worth. This proves to be the single most important lesson you can take from your undergraduate curriculum. You are the artist and you must not only create the masterpiece, but also guide your readers into the correct interpretation of your work as well.

Student Counsel
3L Tom Devine says, "I thought I had writing down to a T, then I came to law school and found out that I needed to start the learning process all over again to write in the style of law."

It is extremely important as an incoming law student to take your undergraduate writing experiences with a grain of salt. The law school writing curriculum is a unique experience. You must realize that law professors will expect a different level of writing and a different finished product. Every word is a weapon. There is no space for wasted thoughts and repetitious words, because each and every word you use in your writing is an opportunity to be a successful law student.

While the transition from a successful collegiate writer to a successful 1L writer may be extremely challenging and difficult, here is a list of what you should and should not take from your undergraduate experience to your new writing curriculum in law school.

What Should You Remember from College?

Solid editing wins. Do not forget the sound editing, grammar, and punctuation skills you polished during your undergraduate experience, as 1L writing calls for the same attention to the English language as collegiate writing.

Avoid redundancies. Remember that your collegiate professors did not appreciate redundant sentences and arguments. Your 1L professors will be particularly irked by redundancies. Clear and concise writing always wins.

Be patient. Remember that the writing process calls for patience. As with collegiate writing, 1L writing will be challenging and at times, you will need to take time away from your work and return later with a fresh mind.

Answer the question. Remember to answer the question asked. As with collegiate writing, 1L assignments will ask a very particular question and require a very particular answer. Do not deviate. Meet the question head on and be direct and straightforward.

Use your resources. Always remember that the professors, whether in college or law school, want to help you succeed. Meet with them regularly, ask questions vigorously, and turn in drafts for edits early. Use every resource at your disposal!

What Should You Forget from College?

Abstract writing. 1L professors appreciate thought and thinking that is outside of the box, but they want clear and concise arguments to support this thinking. Be careful with abstract thinking, as it has the tendency to be ambiguous and vague.

Narrative writing. As a 1L writer, you cannot write papers as a narrator. You have to present arguments in a direct format. You cannot narrate facts. Direct and straightforward techniques always win in law school.

Passive writing. In college, many teachers let you get away with passive writing. In law school, you have to be an active writer searching for the strongest way to persuade your readers to agree with your points. Persuasion is the number one goal of law school writing and it is your responsibility to make every word a persuasive tool.

One-sided arguments. In undergraduate programs, most teachers ask you to pick a side and argue for that side. Writing is different in law school. While professors ask for you to take a side and argue it, they also expect you to explore the other side of the story and the weaknesses in your proposed argument. Always remember that no argument is flawless, and finding the holes in your argument will only help you address them.

What's the Big Difference?

The easiest way to illustrate the difference between undergraduate writing and law school writing is by analyzing actual excerpts from a college writer and a law school writer. The following are two samples of writing, the first of which I wrote as an undergraduate in my senior year and the second of which I wrote as a first-year law student. While there were only four months between the two excerpts, the difference is day and night. The first excerpt came from a persuasive paper dealing with commodification and the television series *The Sopranos,* while the second work is an excerpt from the statement of the case of a law school brief dealing with covenants not to compete. Two of the biggest changes that a growing legal writer needs to address are the persuasiveness of his writing and the reduction of wordiness throughout his briefs. Notice the difference in both of these issues as you read through each piece of work.

Undergraduate Writing

While Tony's questionable treatment of women seems relatively uneventful in the scheme of his life, there are times when this negative commodification causes great remorse and trials for Tony and friends. In the third season of the show, Tony befriends a beautiful art dealer named Valentina and quickly becomes excessively attracted to her. He buys her jewelry, takes her to fancy meals, and uses her for sex. She is first attracted to his money and power, but then finds herself falling in love with the mob boss. However, Tony feels differently and sends her his infamous diamond pin with his regards and goodbyes. The young lady receives his "present" and goes crazy. She tells him he disrespected her and she cannot be bought off like the rest of his whores (Chase, *The Sopranos*). What began as another innocent relationship for Tony turns into tragedy when, while cooking for Tony, Valentina's robe catches on fire from the stove and she becomes engulfed in flames. This greatly affected Soprano. He attempted to commodify this woman's feelings and his actions backfired and created unwanted guilt and remorse, which were far from equal to the time he spent with her. He almost ruined his marriage, he had to increase his Prozac dosage, and he felt great guilt for the woman's debilitating injury, all because he insulted her with his belief that women are objects and can be commodified. Avid watchers of the show see Tony's extra-marital affair become an unavoidable time bomb which leads to excessive sadness on Tony's behalf.

1L Writing

Appellant Emerald Legacy is a cooking personality in Milwaukee who does demonstrations for large national conventions in his kitchen at Legacy on the Lake. Further, Emerald is president of Emerald Inc., which oversees all of his ventures in the restaurant and cooking industries, including his newest cookbook, *An Evening with Emerald* (R. 44).

Emerald hired Appellee Jayme Olive in July 1999 as a sous chef for one of his restaurants, Superior (R. 45). When hired, Jayme was attending the Culinary Program at Brown College. After the job offer, Olive left school early to join Emerald's company to gain further experience in the industry (R. 76). Jayme immediately realized success and in June 2000 was promoted to sous chef at Legacy on the Lake (R.45). There, Olive's primary responsibility was food preparation for the restaurant, but occasionally, when Legacy held cooking demos, Olive prepped the ingredients for the show. Olive's college training, as well as his prior work experience, provided him with necessary skills to perform these basic tasks. Olive received little training from Emerald and acquired most of his skills from chefs at his former jobs (R. 45, 76).

In addition to his ability to perform basic food prep, Olive has a comedic personality and previously did standup in Milwaukee and Chicago (R. 76). Because of his ability to prep food and entertain a crowd, in March 2001 Olive was promoted to Emerald's "warm-up" act for his demos. Before each demo Olive prepped the set and joked with the crowd for about fifteen minutes (R. 46). Olive's "fifteen minutes of fame" was the only exposure received from Emerald. Once his "warm-up" act ended, Olive left the set and only returned when Emerald needed more supplies.

A Tale of Two Styles

These works should begin to illustrate the large difference between undergraduate writing and 1L writing. The styles are totally different. Here are some differences to note:

Be concise: 1L writing calls for less wordiness and more straightforward and concise points.

Use precedent: 1L writing must be based on facts. There is no room for abstract statements and hypothesizing. Concise points supported by case law win the game.

Use your resources correctly: 1L writing requires students to pick and choose their resources. Undergraduate writing often presents the idea that more resources are better. This is not the case in law school. There is plenty of case law out there. The trick is picking the most useful and fact analogous case law for your specific topic.

Edit, edit, edit: In undergraduate programs, students may be able to get away with one strong edit. However, law school students will be faced with making multiple edits, rewrites, and drafts. Be prepared for these and allow the necessary time for each draft.

Short points: In law school, students must make their points in a concise manner. No carrying on. Follow the process the professors teach in class.

Avoid redundancy: Law school professors hate redundant statements. They will often stop reading your paper and take a deep breath when they see them. Undergraduate professors allow students a little more leeway with repetition.

What to Expect as a 1L Writer

As mentioned previously, the first-year curriculum calls for you to write a lot. While understanding theories and analyzing the way these theories operate in our everyday legal lives is extremely important, your knowledge and understanding of the information is always illustrated and tested through essay writing.

Memos

To begin with, most law schools will require you to take at least one writing course during your first year of law school. This first-year writing course usually calls for you to write a twenty- to thirty-page paper typically referred to as a memo. While this word means little to an incoming law student such as yourself, halfway through your first semester in law school, you will cringe at the whisper of the word *memo*. However, that does not have to be the case. While a memo is a challenging and involved paper that calls for you to analyze and argue a specific legal topic, it does not have to be an agonizing experience and can be a great way to display your writing skills.

Memos usually begin with the professor handing out the assignment. This will consist of a large fact pattern that encompasses a legal dispute between two parties. The fact pattern will outline the two parties and their disagreement with one another. It may also contain supporting documents such as contractual agreements between the two parties, or even interviews with both the plaintiff and the defendant. The fact pattern then presents a narrow legal issue that can be argued for both the plaintiff and the defendant. This is where you step in.

In fact patterns, there is often no clear-cut winner and the issue can be split down the middle, so you have the freedom to pick the party you feel you have the best chance of successfully supporting and presenting a case for. It is your responsibility to pick one of the parties, either the plaintiff or the defendant, and argue for them as if you were their hired legal counsel. You must research previous cases with decisions that will both support and refute your arguments, and then organize your thoughts and analyze the situation to create a memo outlining the legal issues and questions. You must then answer those questions in a persuasive and effective manner using unique ideas and strong supporting cases to sway the reader to agree with your case.

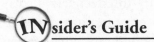 **sider's Guide**

Professor Pointer

Professor Patrick Wiseman says, "Take no shortcuts! There are ways to be efficient in the study of law and the writing process, but shortcuts (such as case briefs and sharing research) are, in the long run, inefficient and will make a student a worse lawyer (especially if, as is sometimes the case for a bright student, the shortcuts seem to work). Do all your own research and writing as this will prepare you to be an educated and intelligent attorney."

Memos are complicated and call for a great deal of energy and meticulous editing. There are usually page limits and deadlines to each memo and you only have a limited amount of time and space to present the strongest case possible for your "client." That being said, it is imperative to ask yourself while writing: "Is this word necessary?" "Is there a shorter way to say what I just said?" "Have I already made this point?" "Do I need to make this point?" All of these questions will help you meet the page requirements you are faced with without losing your content.

Exams

In addition to memo writing, another time you will use your writing skills is during your exams for each casebook-based course. Exam skills and writing techniques are discussed in great detail elsewhere, but it is important to note that exams will rarely allow you time to focus on your writing techniques. The most beneficial thing you can do on an exam is to get it all out. Make all of your points and discuss all of the issues addressed in the exam question. It is rare that professors take points away for addressing unimportant topics, or carrying on about a specific point. The worst thing you can do is not put something on the paper.

During exams, write as quickly as you can, say as much as you need to say, do not worry about the persuasiveness of your writing, and do not worry about whether your word choice is correct 100 percent of the time. A professor is concerned that you understand the concepts, and that you have the ability to effectively display your knowledge. Generally, professors do not care that your sentence structure is not perfect. Whether you do know whether you use weather for the climate or whether for a distinction, the important thing is not your word choice, but whether you can strongly illustrate your grasp on the material. However, it is still important to know your audience. Some professors do harp on word choice and spelling. Always remember to adjust to your professor's likes and dislikes.

Class-Specific Papers

A final type of writing you might be faced with involves papers for specific courses. These courses are generally exam-based courses, but the professor may also require you to write a paper during the course of the semester. These papers can range in topic from the interpretation of an important statute to the research and writing of a paper concerning a specific line of case law. While these papers are not nearly as time-consuming and frustrating as a memo or brief, they still present their own set of challenges and require their own due diligence.

Approach these papers with a unique and original thought process. Professors want to see how well you interpret certain rules and laws that are imperative to the course. Look at the topic from a number of angles, present strong precedent to support your claims, and be clear, concise, and straightforward in your paper. Keep in mind that professors will be reading fifty to seventy-five papers a semester and the last thing they want to read is the same thing over and over again. Be original and unique, and separate yourself from the bunch. Think about it like this: All law schools grade on a curve. If you have the same perspective and thought process as every other student when you are writing your paper, the professor will have no choice but to compare your perspective and paper to every other one he grades. This will make it more difficult to succeed, because the competition increases. However, if your ideas are unique and different, the professor will look at your paper and your perspectives in their own light and based their own worth. Be unique and different; it will give you one more advantage in the fierce competition of the first year.

Professors will usually assign these papers in the beginning of the semester, sometimes as early as the first few weeks. This gives students a chance to get a head start on the papers. Take this head start and run with it. I cannot tell you how big a mistake it is to procrastinate with this assignment. Exams approach faster than you can imagine and the last thing you want to deal with is writing a paper in addition to studying for all of your exams.

These papers are opportunities to nail a good grade and get things moving in the right direction. It is extremely comforting going into your exam knowing that a piece of your grade is already decided in your favor. Take advantage of this paper-writing opportunity to reduce some of the stress and challenges exams will present.

The Writing Process

So you have the assignment, now what do you do? There a few steps you will need to take to ensure your writing is well thought out and concise.

The first step to completing any assignment is actually obtaining it. By this time you have received your assignment from your teacher and are ready to begin thinking about it. Always remember that once you receive an assignment, the sooner you begin to plan your course of action, the better. The best opportunity to ask questions and gain clarification on tough issues is in the beginning of the process, not toward the end. Follow these helpful steps as soon as you can after receiving your assignment.

Sit Down and Think about It

As with any project, the best way to begin is by sitting down, reading the assignment, and thinking about what the professor is asking you to accomplish. Most assignments are long and complicated, and the best step you can take is to sit in front of your computer and break down the assignment into pieces. Figure out exactly what each piece of the assignment is asking you to do. This will make your experience a lot easier, because you will be more organized and you will be tackling small pieces of the puzzle instead of the whole thing at once.

This is a time for you to organize the entire assignment into manageable parts. It will also allow you to better plan your time and avoid procrastination. It is extremely hard to see exactly what you are dealing with when it is a four-page scramble of words. Remember that every statement in the assignment is there for a reason. By breaking down the assignment and thinking about it, you are better equipped to find the value in each piece of the puzzle. If you are not sure what the question is asking, then it is virtually impossible to succeed when you try to answer it.

To begin with, sit down and read through the question. Highlight any new issues with a different colored highlighter. After doing this, list each issue you find and put the pertinent points in the question under the issue. This will allow you to work through the research in an organized and manageable manner. This is a great starting point, and the sooner you are organized, the easier the writing process will be.

Researching the Topic

After you think about the question and organize it, it is important to begin to answer each part of the assignment. The best way to do this is through researching each topic. As a first-year writer, you must be able to research the information you need to support the arguments presented in your writing. Two widely used Web sites are *www.LexisNexis.com* and *www.Westlaw.com.* These are the two predominant search engines students use to research case law. These two Web sites are extremely powerful and useful tools for researching case law and finding decisions that support your clients' cases. For your first memo-writing experience, you will spend hours scouring these two Internet databases to find the most helpful and synonymous cases that will further your argument. Most law schools offer Lexis and Westlaw training in the first few months of semester, so you should not worry; this training will prepare to use these two search engines efficiently.

Now that you have your issues broken down into manageable pieces, it is time to find the answers. It is always wise to do the research and then form your arguments. The reason is that arguments are flexible, while precedent and case law are not. While you search through case after case, you will slowly form your arguments based on the black letter law. It will be a waste of time to form an argument if you cannot find the precedent to support your claim. Have an idea of what you want to argue as you look through the case law, but do not spend a great amount of time forming arguments until you find all of the possible support for your potential claims.

The easiest thing to do is go through issue by issue and find the relevant case law. Once you do this, organize it and pull out the pertinent information. This will allow you to see the big picture and understand exactly how all the precedents fit together.

Using the Case Law

Once you have found all the necessary cases, the next step is to brief them. Just like you are preparing for a class, brief each and every case you find to be important. Briefing the cases will accomplish a few things. To begin with, you will be organized and can easily reference each case you have read. Second, you will save an enormous amount of time because you will not have to constantly refer back to the long cases, since you will have all the information you need on each one of your case briefs. You will be faced with an extremely large number of cases and it will be a lot easier to refer to a single-page brief as opposed to a twenty-page case. Briefing each case also forces you to ask yourself exactly what each case is trying to say. The thought process involved in case briefing forces you to find the issues and support that the court uses when making its decision. This makes you really ask yourself how each case will fit into your assignment and strengthen or weaken your argument.

Once you have organized each case by briefing them, organize them by issue. Since you already broke down each issue in the question, it is now time to start finding the answers. Number each issue you found and go through each and every case and place a corresponding number on the top of each brief so you will immediately know which case law corresponds to which issue. This will save time and maintain your organization throughout the writing process.

Outline, Outline, Outline

After you have completed all of your research and have enough information to answer all of the issues you found, it is time put the information into an outline. Outlining is the most important part of the writing process as you create the skeleton for your paper. This supports your entire work and the rest of the paper is nothing more than filling in the skeleton. The more organized and detailed your outline is, the better. The outline is a road map for the paper and just as with driving, when taking a long trip through many states, the more specific and detailed the driving directions are, the greater the chance that a traveler will get to his or her destination without getting lost. The same is true with legal writing. It is your job to create a well-organized and direct paper in order to guide the reader through the arguments and get them to the right place at the right time.

I always like to start my outline by referring back to my organized issues and case law. Start by placing each one of your issues into outline form. Take each issue (which will usually be directly from the assignment in the form of a question) and turn it into a statement. Each of these statements will be one number on your outline. Once you have the bare bones of the outline with each issue, you can start filling in some of the meat of your outline. Under each issue, write a one- or two-sentence thesis statement. This will answer the question and guide each section of your outline. It is the most important step in the outlining process. The thesis should be a clear and concise answer to the issue based on the research you have done. It should not only answer the issue question, but also guide you in your argument and outline exactly what you will present to your readers.

Once you have created a thesis statement for each issue, begin placing case law into the outline to support your thesis statement. Your thesis statement will be the main argument you are presenting throughout the paper and the case law will support this argument. Always put the most important case law first in your outline because you will rely the most on these arguments. Make sure you cite each case as you place the case law in the outline, as you will always have to reference your work throughout your writing.

After you have placed the case law into your outline to support your thesis, you will also need to address counterarguments. It is extremely important to see other sides of the argument and weaknesses in your own, and this is the perfect time to do just that. You will find opposing case law throughout your research. Go back through each issue and create a counter thesis for your argument. You will then use case law to support the counterarguments. The final step in this process is to refute the counterarguments and demonstrate why your argument is stronger. This is vital to your success as not only a writer, but also as an attorney. To be a successful writer and lawyer, you must be able to identify and understand both sides of the argument. If you can, you will be better prepared and better able to argue your side while preempting your opponent's strategy.

Once you have created a thesis statement for each issue, supported your arguments by case law, and identified the counterarguments, it is now time to create an introduction, conclusion, and fact pattern. The introduction to your memo or brief is similar to any other introduction you have ever done. Outline your main arguments, introduce the essential issues, and guide the readers through your paper. Be clear, concise, and direct because if your readers cannot follow your introduction, they will surely not be able to follow your paper. This is a chance to make a good impression upon your reader. Make sure you take advantage of this opportunity.

Concluding your paper is similar to your introduction, except now you are recapping your essential points and leaving the reader with a summary of your paper. This is the last piece of the puzzle and you should make sure that it completes your entire work. Your conclusion should draw everything together and leave the reader with a sense of closure.

Furthermore, all memos and briefs require you to write a fact section that presents the fact pattern of the assignment. This section generally summarizes the facts that led to the issues you are arguing. The most important part of this section is figuring out which facts are important and which facts do not help your readers understand the issues. Because you are working with space limitations, it is important to be direct and avoid redundancies in your fact section. The fact section should be one page or less, and each fact should have its own independent relevance

Citations

After each factual statement is inserted into the outline, it is imperative for you to cite where the information came from. Plagiarism is severely punished in law school and many times it happens by accident, with the writer having no intention of copying a published work but doing so because he or she is poorly organized and did not cite the resources in the initial outline. One easy way to cite your resources as you progress through your outline is to take each and every case and legal resource you plan on using and assign a number to each one, then write that number on the front of the first page in large writing. When this is finished, you can easily write the reference number and the page number of each resource next to the factual statement you place in your outline. For example, after placing the statement into your outline, to easily cite a resource for quick reference without taking time away from working on your outline, use this form: (1, p. 20). The first number is a reference to the resource that you individually numbered and the second number is the page number of that resource. This method will give you a quick and easy way to reference your work and prevent plagiarism without taking time away from creating the bulk of the outline.

On Your Mark, Get Set, Write

Now that you have taken the time to organize your assignment, research the issues, and outline your arguments, you are ready to sit down in front of your computer and write your rough draft. Following is a list of steps you should take to effortlessly move through the writing process.

Formatting

Once you are done with the outlining process, it is time to create a rough draft of your paper. To begin with, set your margins, line spacing, font, and font size from the beginning of the paper. This will give you a true representation of exactly how much space you have to work with at any given point in the paper. There is nothing worse than having a finished product and realizing that you used a font size of 11 instead of the assigned font size of 12. Now you have to go back and edit your paper for length. This will prevent unnecessary headaches at the end of the assignment, and will also ensure that you follow all of the guidelines set forth in the assignment.

From Outline to Paper

After you set the correct format for your paper, it is time to create a rough draft from your outline. Your first step should be to create your fact section. This is a great starting point, as every argument you make and every issue you address will be based on the facts of the assignment. Once you complete your fact section, move through each issue you have in your outline. You have already outlined a thesis statement and you already have a supporting bundle of case law, so the hard part is done. The next step is fleshing out your argument. Start with your thesis and support it with strong case law. Then, begin to analyze each piece of case law as it relates to your facts and arguments. You must demonstrate the direct correlation between your case law and the facts with which you are presented. If these two are not analogous, you will have a tough time supporting your arguments with the research you conducted. After you work your way through each one of your issue statements in your outline and make your counterarguments, turn to the introduction and conclusion. I always save these for last because they often change as your arguments progress. There is no way to introduce or recap your paper if you have not written it yet. Finish your paper by tying it together with a strong introduction and a sound conclusion that will grasp the attention of your reader.

Framing Thoughts

As you are writing your paper, it is important to focus on exactly how you are phrasing your arguments. The most important and challenging responsibility of law students is to organize their thoughts in a cohesive manner in order to create a strong mold and foundation for their writing assignments. A student's ability to frame thoughts in legalese is essential to his or her future success as a lawyer. Arguably the most important skill to possess is the ability to create an organized outline based on a thorough thought process with the intention of producing a sound argument. Since the law is such a wide-ranging, broad subject, it is key to narrow thoughts and focus efforts on specific areas of interest that will most efficiently support a particular argument. Outlining generally eliminates tangents and significantly directs your arguments.

Word Choice

Every word is a tool and as you are writing your paper and framing your arguments, it is important to find the value in each word you choose. As many legal students will find, the legalese language can easily be simplified because it is often wordy. There are many times when legalese terms must be used, but when able, writers should choose the simplest language to create the clearest thoughts possible. Another helpful hint you can follow to improve your writing is to use strong verbs and to minimize the use of terms such as *is, are, was,* and *were.* These verbs typically lack force and the use of any form of the verb "to be" often leads to writing in the passive voice, which is another writing form that lacks power.

Phrasing Sentences

If words are pieces of the puzzle, then sentence structure is the border of the puzzle. Sentence structure deals with wordiness, redundancy, and grammar. It often takes legal writers a small paragraph to say what they could have said in just a few sentences. Legal writers are often wordy and use needless language. Through eliminating verbosity in writing, readers benefit in three distinct ways: Argument clarity is enhanced, papers can be read with less effort, and arguments have a greater impact on readers.

Edit, Edit, Edit

The editing process is a way for you to fine-tune your work and put the finishing touches on your masterpiece. The most effective way to do this is with a fresh palate. When you diligently work on your paper for a long period of time, you may have problems focusing on your mistakes and reorganizing your thoughts in a more persuasive and effective manner. However, once you finish your paper and allow time to pass, you can start fresh with the editing process. The editing process is one of the most important parts of any writing process, as this is the time to eliminate poor grammar, sentence structure, and redundancies, and to ensure your argument is strong. You should edit numerous times as the more you edit, the greater chance you will have of finding mistakes within your work.

Writing Made Easy: Easy Tips for Even Easier Writing

Here is a comprehensive list of helpful tips you can use to reduce stress and increase success while writing in your first year of law school. This section also includes examples of a good piece of writing, a better piece of writing, and the best piece of writing.

Adapt to Your Surroundings

My first course in law school was civil procedure. My professor thought the English language was only useful when used correctly. Correct spelling and grammar were important to him and many students felt they received lower marks because they used poor punctuation, grammar, etc. The point is to know your audience and be malleable. Do not get caught in a systematic approach to writing your exams or papers. Be flexible in order to change to fit in the different environments you will encounter, because each and every one of your law school courses will be different. Just like no two snowflakes ever look the same, no two law professors conduct their classrooms in the same way.

Good: A good student receives his first-semester grade and schedules a meeting with the professor to discuss how he could improve his work and his grade for the next semester.

Better: A better student pays attention in class to pick up on professor cues and tailors his work toward the professor's liking.

Best: The best student meets with the professor early on in the course. He finds out exactly what the professor likes and implements this information into his work. He takes practice tests and meets with the professor to go over his writing and to review how he can improve his work for the next time around.

Preparation Is Key

Always remember that solid preparation and planning will solve many of the challenges you face in your first year. Preparation is the best preventive medicine. In law school, and especially in the writing curriculum, preparation will usually cure the majority of your problems. Legal writing requires great amounts of planning and preparation in the form of outlines and research. Therefore, proper preparation before you begin the writing process will ensure success throughout the writing process.

Good: A good student outlines all of her work before she writes anything.

Better: A better student outlines all of the issues she is faced with. She outlines all the potential answers to each and every issue and creates a well-prepared, organized outline.

Best: The best student creates an outline right after the assignment is given out. Then she schedules a meeting with her professor to go over her outline before she begins writing. This saves time and effort and puts her in a position to write a successful paper.

Watch Out for Writing Restraints

Writing assignments in law school place different restraints on the writer, including space and time limitations. Repetition and unnecessary wordiness are the greatest obstacles an incoming law student must overcome to succeed as a writer. Each word you use should have a purpose. Use your words wisely and reduce your phrasing of sentences to the lowest common denominator.

Good: A good student uses a thesaurus and avoids redundancies in his writing. He goes through each paragraph and edits the paragraph to end on a full line instead of a few words to save space.

Better: A better student writes his paper without regard to space. He then goes back through every phrase and asks, "Is this the most concise way I can say this?" After this step, he replaces his wordiness with concise, clear writing.

Best: The best student takes all of the previously mentioned steps, but he also ranks his arguments by importance and puts the most space restraints on the least important arguments. He finds value in each word and avoids all redundancies, as they waste a ton of space and add nothing to the paper.

Quick Tip

Once you receive your writing assignment, take the guidelines list and turn it into a numbered checklist. As you meet each one of the guidelines on your checklist, check them off to ensure you have followed each one. Another step writers can take when they are over their length requirement is to end each paragraph on a full line. You should always end a paragraph on the farthest possible point of the line. Paragraphs with one word on the last line are a waste of almost twelve words. This is an easy way to save almost four lines on a page, which can add up to a great deal of extra space to work with on a thirty-page memo.

Grammar

In addition to reducing excessive verbosity, it is also vital to your success to focus on simple grammar skills such as avoiding passive voice; keeping the subject, verb, and object of the sentence together; and ending sentences emphatically. Passive voice is a display of weak writing. By making the sentence active, you place emphasis on the subject and you can create a more powerful argument. Furthermore, make sure the subject, verb, and object remain together in your sentences. By placing the action at the beginning of sentences, readers will be pleased and more responsive to the style of your writing. A final step you should take to drastically improve the readability and quality of your work is ending sentences emphatically. Especially with considerably longer sentences, writers often lose persuasiveness as the sentences come to a close. End sentences with a special kick. By ending sentences emphatically, you leave your readers with the most important points and hold readers' interest throughout long arguments.

Good: A good student follows all grammar rules, uses spell check and grammar check, and proofreads her work before turning it in.

Better: A better student follows all grammar laws, asks for outside editing, and double-checks for passive voice.

Best: The best student finishes her paper, edits it herself, and uses others to edit. She ensures her sentences end emphatically and that they are readable. Her paper is interesting and holds the reader's attention.

Quick Tip

It is difficult to pinpoint every grammar mistake you make in your paper. However, if you have a number of additional eyes on your paper, this will ensure that all the mistakes have been corrected. Assign different parts of your paper to different "eyes," so they can better focus on the grammar in their specific section.

Simple and Concise Is Better

Simplifying wordy phrases adds power to your writing. There are many overused phrases in the English language that can easily be simplified. There are countless synonyms in the English language. Concise writing leads to successful writing. Finding the most clear and succinct way to make a point will really save you time and effort in the long run. You will have to edit less and you will have more space to flesh out complicated arguments. When you are standing in front of a judge and representing your client, the judge will grow impatient if you ramble on and seem unprepared. However, if you know your arguments and present them in a concise manner, you will be ahead of the game and the judge will not only appreciate this, but will also listen more carefully. The same is true when you are writing. Professors are likely to give you the benefit of the doubt and to be more receptive to your arguments when you use fewer, more carefully chosen words.

Good: A good student replaces wordy sentences and phrases with concise writing.

Better: A better student looks for simplicity in his writing. He reduces his writing to the least common denominator and asks his editors if they can reduce his language to an even simpler, more reader-friendly version.

Best: The best student takes all of the steps mentioned previously, but goes one step further. He uses his thesaurus on any sentence that seems wordy. Before he begins writing, he also creates a list of wordy language so as he writes he can avoid using any words on his "wordy list."

Quick Tip

When you are writing, put a thesaurus next to your computer or use Shift +F7 on your PC keyboard so you will always have a synonym at your fingertips. Also double-check the definition in a dictionary before using the word, because even though they are "synonyms," they aren't necessarily interchangeable in every context.

Write as a Speaker

A final tip you can implement in your writing is to make sure your writing can be effortlessly spoken. Judge Jerome Frank once said, "The primary appeal of the language is to the ear. Good writing is simply speech heightened and polished." A great lesson can be learned from Judge Frank's understanding of writing. When a writer's words are clear and easily spoken, readers feel a stronger connection with the material and feel as if they are part of the work. When legal students strive to implement these tools into their everyday work, only then will they reach their goals as first-rate writers.

Good: A good student uses contractions sporadically so as to increase the readability of his work. This will provide his reader with a more reader-friendly sentence structure.

Better: A better student uses contractions and asks others to edit the paper for readability and the use of easily spoken language.

Best: The best writer takes all the tips previously mentioned. When she is finished with her paper, she reads it aloud to her peers and makes the necessary recommendations and changes to ensure her work is spoken effortlessly.

Quick Tip

Reading your paper aloud to others allows those listening to you to stop you when the writing does not flow clearly.

Saving Space

Even if you can implement all of these helpful hints, if you cannot do it in the allotted space then you may have won the battle, but you will lose the war. Each assignment you receive in law school will not only test your ability to answer the question, but it also will ask you to do so with the weight of a space restraint upon your back. Many professors will even deduct points if you exceed the maximum length requirements. It is imperative to know what limitations you are working with and respect those restraints.

Good: A good student reads the assignment carefully before he begins so he follows all guidelines and writing restraints.

Better: A better student follows all of the guidelines in the assignment and edits at the end. This ensures that he gets his arguments on paper and follows all the necessary guidelines.

Best: The best student writes his paper, edits his work, and then refers back to the assignment and his paper to make sure he followed all the guidelines. He is in contact with the professor and participates and pays attention in class in case the guidelines and length requirements change.

Quick Tip

Set your margins early and place a page number on each page of your work so you know how much more space you have to meet the paper guidelines.

Use Your Editing Resources

Always use the resources around you to help your editing process. View your editing sessions as a surgical procedure. You are a heart doctor with a scalpel in hand and you must trim away the unnecessary pieces of your paper and only leave the useful and helpful information, just as a heart surgeon uses her scalpel to remove harmful disease. Furthermore, as a heart surgeon you have many nurses and other doctors aiding you in the surgical procedure. The same is true as a legal writer. You should surround yourself with colleagues, friends, and family who are willing to help you trim away the unnecessary pieces of your legal writing and produce a concise final product. The most helpful resources you have around you are the people that care about your success. They will offer you the most help and take the editing process seriously. They will not shortchange the editing process and they will be up-front and honest with you and your work product.

Good: A good student finishes her paper and then edits it immediately.

Better: A better student finishes her paper early and steps away from her work so she can edit later. She repeats this process a few times to make sure she caught every mistake.

Best: The best student finishes her work and allows time before editing. She then sends her paper to friends and family for multiple edits, and then edits it herself one more time to ensure her paper is in the best possible form.

Quick Tip

Before you even begin writing, talk to family and friends and assign a part of your paper to each one of them to edit. This will allow direct and more concentrated feedback for smaller sections.

Edit at the End

Edit your paper after you have presented all of your arguments in each section. Editing as you are writing, before you even finish, is challenging because a lot of times editing is like the television show *Survivor*, where you have no choice but to take your weakest ideas and arguments out of your paper. It is extremely difficult to figure out what arguments are the weakest when you have not made all of them. However, once you finish a section or particular argument, go back and assess the value of each argument. Place a numerical value by each one and then go back and see which argument has the lowest value. Begin editing this argument for conciseness and necessity. The biggest mistake a writer can make is cutting out his or her strongest arguments. Play the game of *Survivor* with your paper and keep the strongest arguments to ensure the highest quality of your finished product.

Good: A good student edits after he finishes each section of his paper so that he is focused on his work and can edit one argument at a time.

Better: A better student edits after each argument, but then goes back through the paper at the end and edits the entire work to ensure readability and cohesiveness.

Best: The best student does his editing after each section. He then takes time away from his work and he edits the entire paper for content when he returns. After this, he goes through one final time and edits solely for grammar. Separating edits for grammar and content allows him to focus on one problem area at a time.

Quick Tip

Highlight each one of your arguments with a different colored highlighter so you create a visual representation of the length of each argument. This will allow you to see how you used your space throughout your paper.

Now It's Time to Get Started

Always be confident in your work. Law schools only accept students they feel will excel in their program and eventually become a positive representation of their institution. When you receive your acceptance from a law school, it should be a boost of confidence and motivation. Fear will only decrease the chances of your success. Do not spend time worrying about unnecessary parts of your paper at the wrong time, as it takes useful time away from producing the finest paper possible. Worry about editing when you are editing and worry about researching when you are doing the research. Stay the course and do not allow your mind become engulfed by trepidation when it should be focused on success.

It is important to take the lessons this chapter presents and implement them in your daily writing curriculum. You will be faced with an overwhelming amount of writing as a first-year student, but it is imperative to remember that you can succeed and that you will succeed if you put in the necessary time, work, and effort. Rome wasn't built in a day, and you won't write the perfect memo in just a few hours. It takes time, hard work, and dedication to the law school writing process and the class assignment. Follow the steps outlined in this chapter and you will find that success is just a few helpful hints away.

CHAPTER EIGHT

Distractions: The Good, the Bad, and the Necessary

MARCH 10, 2004

Spring Break

Finally, spring break. I can leave my metaphorical sweat, blood, and I tears behind. I can leave my impending first-year exams behind. I can leave it all behind. I can fall into my black hole of distractions and for one week I can be normal again. Do I even know how to be normal? Is it possible I can even be an active member of society? Has law school sucked my social skills dry and left me a shell of my normal being? I finally have the opportunity to allow my distractions to tempt me. I can finally fall into my temptations and enjoy my distractions. As I sit back in my seat, the woman next to me leans over and looks at the book in front of me and says, "Honey, that law book won't do you any good overseas. Why don't you take a look at this," and she hands me a magazine. I begin to flip through it and allow my distractions take to over the next week of my life. I gently murmur, "Thank goodness for distractions and small favors."

The Balancing Act

At this point, there should be no doubt in your mind that your first year of law school will call for a significant amount of your time and effort. The majority of your life will be spent reading, briefing, and studying. This means two things. First of all, spend most of your time focusing on succeeding during your first year. Second, don't spend all of your time focusing on succeeding during your first year.

Success in your first year will be based as much on what you don't do as on what you do. You should be studying and focusing on the material, but you should also nurse your health, your social life, your mind, and your body in other ways. A piece of the law school formula that students often forget is to rest, relax, and have fun. You have to take breaks, you have to have fun, and you have to get away from it all. There is a time to work and a time to enjoy life! Allow yourself to be distracted. Whether it is a spring break trip or a weekend outing with your significant other, take time off and relax. Distractions often have a negative connotation, but with the stress of law school, distractions are necessary, and they should be viewed in a positive light.

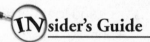

Insider's Guide

Professor Pointer

Professor Roy Sobelson says, "I would encourage students to maintain some balance in their lives. Law school is difficult and quite time-consuming, but it can also consume students in another way, forcing them to spend all of their time thinking about law school and reacting to everything in life like a law student would. Keep that balance by continuing to exercise, enjoying friends and family, and participating in hobbies and the like."

There are three types of distractions during your first year: good distractions, bad distractions, and necessary distractions. Good distractions are those that pull you away from law school, but do so in a rejuvenating fashion to alleviate your law school stress. These distractions are positive because they allow you time away from law school without negatively impacting your study time and focus on your studies. The second type of distraction is one that takes you away from law school and prevents you from studying or preparing for classes and exams. These are considered the bad distractions. Distractions are necessary, but it is your responsibility to choose positive distractions as opposed to those that have negative implications on your schoolwork. The final type of distraction is necessary distractions, which you simply have to participate in to maintain your life and health. These distractions pull you away from law school, but also accomplish an important life task, such as a doctor's appointment or paying your bills. They are necessary to your livelihood and personal maintenance.

I like to look at distractions using the analogy of purchasing a brand-new car and attempting to outfit that car and take care of it. There are good additions to a brand-new vehicle, bad additions, and those additions that are necessary. Once you buy your new car, you need to make some good additions to it. An example of a good addition would be buying new tires to increase the tread life or purchasing a higher grade of gas to increase your mileage and reduce your engine wear. These are similar to good distractions in law school because they help your cause and increase your likelihood of succeeding. Next you decide to make a last-minute purchase and put an expensive radio in your car even though you have not paid your bills this month. This may be similar to a bad distraction because it increases your stress and is completely unnecessary. Finally, you decide to change your oil regularly and always take your car to the shop at the recommended mileage. This is much like a necessary distraction, as it is necessary to preserve your livelihood and the life of your vehicle. While a car and your law school distractions may be completely different, the point is that there are distractions that will fuel your energy and add miles to your ability to endure law school. There are also distractions that will deplete you and drive you down the wrong path.

Time for Distractions

So the question remains: What exactly are positive distractions and how can you use those distractions during your first year as part of your road to success? Distractions are an everyday event and should be used to break up the stress that law school often creates. As a first-year law student, your mind will be put to the test. Every reading session, every case, and every brief will take an inevitable toll on your mind and body. That being said, you have to walk a thin line as a student and allow distractions to be available without abusing them. Distractions can either be a helpful tool in law school or a hurtful one. It all comes down to your discipline and your choices. Distractions are everywhere, whether it be the television downstairs from your study room, the Internet on your computer, or the beautiful weather outside. Whatever the case may be, distractions are simply unavoidable. So while the temptation is present in your life, it is ultimately your choice to either focus on your work, or focus on a distraction. Using distractions as part of your law school formula for success is a two-part process. The first step in the process is to take a look at the best time to use distractions.

The following are the most advantageous and useful times to take advantages of distractions:

In between classes. Classes are not only intense, but will also comprise the majority of your law school days. Most classes last about an hour and a half, but they can run up to three hours if you only meet once a week. Paying attention in class and participating on a daily basis will take a lot out of you. Because of this, it is important to recharge yourself and take a break between classes. If you have two classes back to back, you may not have much time to refresh before the next battle, but you should do the best you can and use the restroom, grab a drink, and maybe take a quick walk outside for a breath of fresh air. If you are lucky enough to have a break between classes, take some time to rejuvenate and recover from your last class. Take a nap, grab a workout on campus, or go have a nice lunch or snack in the afternoon. Doing so will allow you to recover from your last class while recharging you and mentally preparing you for your next class. While you may feel this is a waste of time when you have pages upon pages to read for the next day, you will certainly make up the time because you will be able to focus and work more productively when you begin your work for the next day.

Before bedtime. The last thing you should be doing is reading up until the minute you go to bed. This is a perfect time to fall into those distractions and watch some television or catch up with friends and family. After a long day of law school, you won't have much energy left over, so why push it when you can recharge and relax your mind, which will help you get a goodnight's sleep for the next day. One of the most valuable lessons you will learn is that sometimes the time of day that you study can be as important as how you use that time. When you feel your tank is empty after a long day, use those positive distractions as a way to rest your mind and body.

During long study periods. Law school is a marathon and not a sprint. Because of this, you will find that you have studied longer and harder than ever. More times than not you will sit down with your books and study for hours. I found it helpful to schedule my study time in three-hour blocks with an hour off for distractions. I could wake up and study from 9 A.M. to 12 P.M., and then take an hour break and take my dog for a walk or have a relaxing meal. Distractions are imperative during your marathon study sessions, because they refresh your mind. The bottom line is that you will only be able to focus so hard and study for so long. The trick to successful studying is to find a happy medium between rest and reading. Read until you need rest, and then focus on your distractions and allow them to provide some release from the stress studying can often create. Do not allow yourself to overstudy without taking a break; this will save you time on the front end but cost you the ability to focus on and learn the material on the back end, as you will be out of gas.

During your exam period. Dealing with distractions during your exam period will be one of the largest obstacles you will face during your first year. You are balancing two contravening forces. On one hand, you have a lot of information to review and learn, and it takes a great deal of time to properly study it. On the other hand, you have a lengthy exam period and do not want to burn yourself out or overstudy early on. Thus, taking breaks between exams and during study periods is extremely important to successful exam preparation. It is easy to become overly distracted because of the amount of time you will spend in front of your books, but the key is to view distractions like you view studying: Make time for them and focus your efforts on them as well. When you are taking a break, focus on your distractions and allow yourself to forget about the stress of law school. Whether you are studying or relaxing, the most important thing is to focus on whatever you are doing, because studying can be a distraction just like anything else.

During the holidays. The holidays present an interesting situation. They allow you large chunks of time away from law school, but usually fall right before exams begin. Thanksgiving break usually comes right about the time you should start studying heavily for exams. Thus, you should take time off and spend that time with your family and friends, but you must also focus on your law school responsibilities and ensure you are prepared for your upcoming exams. The most wonderful part of your first year of law school is that final few minutes of your last exam before winter break. You can finally leave the law school and forget about all your worries and concerns and focus on your distractions and all the parts of your life you have put on the shelf during your first semester of law school. Take the time to enjoy your holiday breaks; they are generally the quiet before one hell of a storm.

During your breaks. Winter break and spring break are times for yourself. You should have few, if any, concerns about law school during these breaks. Your exams are over, or at least far enough away that you shouldn't be overly concerned about them, and you finally have some time to indulge your temptations and enjoy the distractions you have avoided for so long. These breaks are great times to spend time with your family and friends and even take a trip. There isn't a better feeling than hopping on a flight and visiting old college friends in a new city. Take advantage of these breaks. They are perfect opportunities to recharge and fill up your tank before law school becomes a reality once again.

On the weekends. The weekends are a great time to catch up on sleep, errands, cleaning, friendships, family, and whatever else you didn't have time for during the week. Since you will not have class on the weekends, sleep in and catch up on any work you didn't do during the week. After you accomplish these responsibilities, take some time and enjoy your distractions. Enjoy the weekends and refresh yourself for the upcoming week.

Each of the opportunities mentioned previously are great times to focus on your distractions and take a step away from law school. Law school is an endless balancing act and will challenge every facet of your life. Distractions allow you a break from this challenge and an opportunity to recharge and rejuvenate. The trick is finding the correct time to do so. It is no mystery that you need distractions to divert your attention from the stress of law school. The mystery lies in how exactly to do this. The previous discussion should help you decipher this mystery and paint a picture of when you should be focusing on your distractions and when you should be taking a break from law school. No matter what you hear from your fellow students and professors, distractions are necessary and vital to your first-year success.

The Good Distractions

The beginning of this chapter discussed the first part of the "distraction equation," that is, finding time for your distractions. Once you have a feeling for when you should allow yourself to be distracted, it is vital to use this time in a positive manner. Distractions are necessary, but can also be detrimental if used incorrectly. If you have a tough exam the next day, the last thing you should be doing is going out with friends and partying until late in the evening, regardless of whether your exam is in the morning, afternoon, or evening. A better approach would be to grab a few friends and enjoy a movie or a glass of wine with dinner. The way you are distracted is just as important as the time you dedicate to your distractions. This section will focus on positive distractions and the time you should use them, while the next section will focus on negative distractions and their implications.

Student Counsel

3L Jerimiah Jarmin says, "Distractions are definitely necessary. The human mind and body were not designed to sit
sedate for eight hours a day. This decreases one's ability
to comprehend and digest material and reduces efficiency.
Take time to work out, enjoy a movie, or go out occasionally
with your friends."

Take a look at the following types of positive distractions and the
most appropriate times to use them during your first year:

Holidays

Holidays are extremely important to your law school sanity.
They are a wonderful time to catch up with family and friends
and enjoy a break from law school. You may be an out-of-state law
student with friends and family in other states. Make sure you can
find the time to get away from the university and spend time with
your family during the holidays. You will feel sad and left out, and
regret not going home if you have the chance to do so. Go home,
study on the flight, and take the holiday off so you have a break
from your law school responsibilities. Recharge and when you get
back to school, focus on law school once again.

Vacations

Vacations are a great opportunity for a change of scenery. There
are very few times when you will have the ability to leave town
and really get away from law school for an extended period, but
I strongly suggest that you do so when you can. Vacations allow
you to truly escape and focus on all of your distractions without
the worry of law school. Vacations are great during spring break
and winter break, but if you stay on top of your work and remain
focused during the week, it is not totally out of the question to

take a quick trip on the weekend, so long as it is the middle or beginning of the semester and nowhere near exams.

Insider's Guide

Attorney Advice

Attorney Sarah Kass says, "I think some distractions are necessary in law school. If you spend three years doing nothing but preparing for class and exams, you will drive yourself, and everyone around you, crazy. You have to remember that you have friends and family outside of law school and give them the time and attention they deserve. Our first semester exams were the week after Thanksgiving. I stayed in Atlanta for the holiday, rather than go home to celebrate with my family. Though I did study a lot, I regretted not going home to be with my family as they were all celebrating and eating turkey together. I soon realized that though I needed to devote a lot of time to school, I was not willing to jeopardize spending time with the people I loved. After that holiday, I made more time for friends and family and found that I could better tolerate law school with them as a much needed distraction."

Significant Others

Your spouse or significant other will provide you with great distractions from the everyday stress and strain of law school. They will nurture you and be there for you when you need to talk. They can always help out in other facets of your life. Whether it be doing some laundry or cooking dinner, they provide you with meaningful support and time savers so you can focus your efforts on law school. Significant others are a positive distraction. They are your number one supporters and will always be willing to help you and reinforce the goals you are trying to achieve during your first year of law school.

Attorney Advice

Attorney Sara Barker says, "I found my boyfriend to be a wonderful distraction and a helpful part of my life, even though we were in the exact same boat since we were classmates. People often warn against dating a classmate. I, however, found myself in a relationship with a classmate by the first week of school. While during finals we may not have had much else to talk about except what we had studied that day, it made it much easier to have a relationship with someone who was going through the same experience as me, since my first year of law school completely consumed my life. Also, it was great to have someone to count on to study with and keep me sane during exams. On the negative side, if it doesn't work out, you do have to see that person every day for the next three years, so be wary of jumping into a relationship with a classmate unless you can see it lasting."

Movies

Movies were always one of my favorite distractions during my first year of law school for a few reasons. They allow a meaningful escape from law school in the sense that they take your mind off of everything and truly distract you from the stress of law school. You will easily be enthralled with the storyline and forget about all your anxieties and stress for a few hours. They are also easy to fit into your schedule at your own convenience. Movies are great distractions to use at night after your studies or on the weekends when you have more time on your hands. Try to pick a movie that is not emotionally draining, but rather a romantic comedy or an action flick, as they won't tug at your emotions and leave you exhausted at the end. Whatever the case may be, pick your distraction, grab a bag of popcorn, and relax on the couch and let your mind wander.

Workouts

Working out is quite possibly the most therapeutic type of distraction. It alleviates stress and relaxes your body. Law school will give you tense shoulders and a sore neck. A workout will relax your tense posture and drastically reduce your everyday stress. Most universities have gyms on campus, so you can quickly pop in and out of them during an extended lunch hour or a break in your afternoon schedule. Working out is a fantastic distraction because of the ease with which you can partake of it. Whether your workout is a jog through the park, lifting weights in the gym, Pilates, yoga, walking your dog, a brisk walk around the university between classes, or a pickup game of basketball, take advantage of your time to work out, as it will keep your mind and body strong and healthy during your first year of law school.

Meals

Breakfast, lunch, and dinner are great opportunities for distractions, as they are multipurpose. They fulfill an everyday need and also take you away from your law school stress. I always found it useful to have lunch or dinner with friends so I had an opportunity to catch up with people I had probably taken for granted for a few days. Going out for dinner is a wonderful way to do this, because it gets you away from the books and out of the house for an hour or two. As obvious as it may be, whether you take long breaks or short ones for meals, make sure you eat regularly and stay healthy. Law school is hard enough without a terrible cold or the flu. Avoiding fast foods and eating healthy will increase your energy and allow you to better focus on your responsibilities when you need to.

Family and Friends

Family and friends are your support group. They want to see you succeed and want to hear about it every step of the way. Your friends and family are your law school lifeline. While it may be challenging, do not take them for granted and try your hardest to make time for them. When you are down, they will pick you up and when you are stressed, they will calm your nerves. Invest in your friends and family during your first year and don't lose sight of what is important. Remember, they need you as much as you need them. The best way to stay on track and make time for this distraction is to take one night a week and have dinner with your family and friends. Work hard during the day so you can take a few hours off and focus on those you love and care about.

Television

Television was always my haven. I would work hard during the day and set my TiVo to record all of my favorite shows at night. Once I completed my work, I would grab the remote and lie in bed and enjoy this distraction. I would also recommend signing up for TiVo or DVR when you call for cable. It costs a few extra bucks, but drastically reduces the time you spend in front of a television as you bypass all the commercials. Imagine that you watch two one-hour shows every night after your schoolwork. By using a DVR, you save close to 25 percent of the time by bypassing all the commercials. That gives you an extra thirty minutes to brief a case, catch a few extra Zs, or even watch an extra show. Television relaxes your mind before you fall asleep and generally fits in your schedule, and there is always something entertaining on the tube. While television does present a positive distraction that is readily available, you have to be careful—because it is readily available. It is quite easy to flip on the tube while you are studying and get lost in a program for hours on end. Television is great, but make sure you use it at appropriate times, namely, after you have finished all of your other responsibilities.

Shopping

Shopping is a wonderful distraction for first-year law school students. Whether it is shopping for groceries, clothes, or other incidentals, it is always healthy to take some time outside of the house to accomplish responsibilities other than those associated with law school. Shopping is quick and easy and the mere process of focusing your mind and efforts on other tasks will provide a much needed and quite useful distraction. I always found it useful to do my grocery shopping on the weekend for the upcoming week so I didn't have to worry about meals or snacks while focusing on the grueling week I was in the midst of. As great a break as shopping can be, keep your budget in mind and don't overspend, as bills can pile up quickly and create even more stress than you already have.

Reading and Writing

A final distraction you should consider during your first year is outside reading and writing. You will spend the majority of your time during your first year of law school in front of books, but I always found it relaxing to grab a magazine and read through it before I went to bed. As a leisure activity, I also practiced my creative writing during my first year of law school, which I enjoyed because it was extremely different from memo or brief writing. While reading and writing may not seem like the best distraction from the extensive reading and writing in law school, I would suggest that if you were an avid reader before law school, do not give up this valuable distraction just because you are in law school. Reading and writing outside of law school will keep your senses sharp and your mind relaxed while distracting you from the intense curriculum you are faced with each and every day.

Whatever your distraction of choice may be, there are endless ways to alleviate the stress and strain associated with your everyday law school experiences. Law school calls for your diligence and the majority of your time. However, as a first-year student, you must balance the hard work with the countervailing distractions. Finding the happy medium may be the most challenging task that you will face during your first year. The key to success is using your distractions in a meaningful and appropriate manner. Distractions should be breaks from study sessions. They should provide you with a significant change from your everyday activities. Using these distractions to accomplish important life tasks such as eating, sleeping, relaxing, or working out will help keep your mind and body healthy and happy.

The Bad Distractions

While positive distractions will alleviate the stress and strain of law school, negative distractions will create more stress in the end. They may start as wonderful ideas and healthy breaks from your first year but end up adding unnecessary pressure in your life. You simply do not have time for extra headaches. There is no need to bring further complications into your life, as you will have enough anxiety with those created by your professors and the first-year curriculum.

I once heard a story that will illustrate this point. A few first-year law students decided to take a trip right before their upcoming midterm. They had studied hard and felt it was time for a distraction. Instead of grabbing a movie or a night on the town, they decided to drive to Vegas for the weekend. Their midterm was set to begin at 1 P.M. on the following Monday. On Friday they left town and hit Vegas hard. They partied, gambled, and stayed up late into the night. On Sunday night they planned on going to bed early and waking up the next morning to head back to school. At the last minute they were invited to a grand-opening party at Pure, the hottest club in Vegas. They decided to attend and partied all night, waking up at noon the next day, only an hour before their midterm. They drove back the second they awoke, but were still late for the exam. They went to the professor's office and decided to lie to her and tell her they had a flat tire heading back from a weekend trip to the mountains. This was obviously a lie and the professor was on to them. She agreed to the give them a makeup exam the next day. They arrived at school and were given an exam in her office. The exam had one question on it, and in the end, each student failed the exam. The question read: "You stated you had a flat tire on the way back. My question to you is: Which tire?"

The point of this story illustrates how a negative distraction cost these students a grade during their first year. They were unprofessional, irresponsible, and made a poor choice that cost them in the long run. They fell into a negative distraction and paid greatly for it. This story illustrates just one of the potentially negative distractions you may be faced with during your first year. However, there are many other negative distractions that you should avoid during your first year.

Trips

The previous story is a classic example of how vacationing at the wrong time can be a detrimental distraction. Vacations are a wonderful distraction, but should be avoided during the weeks leading up to the exams. Furthermore, it is not a great idea to take trips and miss class during the first weeks of the semester, as this should be a time to find your footing and staying on top of your course work. Whatever the case, whenever you take vacations, you should always use the flights or the car rides (assuming you are a passenger) to study and review your notes from class. Missing class may be one of the hardest obstacles to overcome, so avoid vacations and distractions that pull you away from law school and the accompanying responsibilities.

Nightlife

Nightlife can be a tricky distraction to control. When you are going to school in a big city, there is always an interesting opportunity to get out of the house and have a drink or go to an event. Avoiding these distractions was one of my greatest personal challenges because I was always a socialite in college. I learned quickly that law school is nothing like college and calls for more studying and preparation than college did. My challenge with Atlanta nightlife presents an interesting point. Some distractions will be harder for you to control than others. If you are an avid traveler, it may be considerably more challenging to give up taking trips during the semester. Distractions take many different forms and mean different things to different people. Perhaps you are a popular culture nut and have to attend every movie opening you can. You may have to adjust your practices and catch some of these movies on video. Whatever the case may be, nightlife can be extremely distracting and take away considerable time from your studies.

Alcohol

Alcohol can have a negative effect on your law school performance if used without practicing moderation. I am a realist and I know many first-year law students are recent college grads and enjoy partying. However, drinking will not only take away from studying, but it may also keep you up late at night and affect you the next day if you are tired or have a hangover. By no means am I a proponent for cutting all the partying out of your life as a first-year student, but I do believe you should focus on your schooling and realize why you are there: to succeed. Alcohol can be a negative distraction and drastically affect your performance in your first year.

Drugs

Simply put, there is no place in law school for drug use. There really isn't an argument anyone can make as to the benefits of drug use during law school, or anytime for that matter. Of course, I am referring to illegal drugs as opposed to those drugs prescribed to you by your doctor or therapist. You will need every brain cell you have in your head to succeed in your first year and the last thing you should be doing is breaking the law and killing those brain cells. Furthermore, if you were to get caught using drugs, this would be a major issue during your fitness check when you sit for the BAR. Drugs are a distraction you should never consider.

Television

As great as television can be as a quick and easy distraction, it is so readily available to you that it can become a negative distraction very quickly. There is probably a television located in every room in your house. If you are studying at home, it is so easy to flip on the tube and get hooked on a show. There is always something on the tube, so there is always a negative distraction available. Try to avoid this by studying at school or coffee shops. The best way to avoid a distraction is to eliminate it.

Internet

The Internet will be the most available distraction of the bunch. Even in class you will have access to the Internet. Many students use their laptops to study for exams, take class notes, and review outlines. Thus, the Internet is readily available and can easily pull you away from your focus on law school. While the Internet will provide you with valuable resources like Westlaw and LexisNexis, it also has millions of distractions that you can access with the push of a button. If you do not need the useful resources the Internet may provide, leave the Ethernet cable at home or disable your wireless Internet connection. Once again: out of sight, out of mind. Avoiding negative distractions during your study periods or class sessions will allow you to focus all of your attention on the course material.

Roommates

To have a roommate or to live alone, that is the question. Roommates can be one of the most negative and overbearing distractions in your life during your first year if you do not deal with the situation correctly. For starters, it is imperative to decide if even having a roommate is right for you. Living with another person is a wonderful way to reduce the monthly bills and expenses. Internet, cable, power, electric, and rent are all magically cut in half the moment you sign a lease agreement with a friend. However, the last thing you should do is move in with someone you are not compatible with to save money. If you can, live alone. It reduces the stress and creates fewer distractions. Who knows when your buddy will want to have a housewarming party or invite a few people over to watch a movie? Most of these problems vanish instantaneously if your roommate is a fellow 1L. If that is the case, your roommate will be in the same boat as you and simply won't have to time to be a distraction.

I went through six different roommates during my law school career, one of which was a beautiful little puppy named Guinness. It wasn't because I was a bad roommate or they were bad roommates; it was just because they had different responsibilities and different circumstances. The point is that if you are financially fortunate enough to have the opportunity to live alone, you only have to account for yourself and do not have to be worried about a dirty apartment, a late-night gathering, or food magically disappearing from the fridge. Keep in mind that you know your lifestyle better than anyone else does. If you find that living with other people is not distracting and is actually a necessary positive in your life, go for it.

After reviewing the sections on the difference between negative distractions and positive distractions, the fine line between them should be clear. A positive distraction can quickly become a negative one if abused. Thus, the trick is walking the line and ensuring you are focusing on the positive distractions at appropriate times. There is a time and place for everything during your first year, including distractions of all forms. Make sure you use your distractions in a positive manner to benefit and aid in your preparation for exams instead of hurting your first-year success.

The Necessary

Necessary distractions are different from those distractions mentioned in the previous section. They cannot be classified as good or bad distractions, but rather are necessary to your well-being. These distractions take you away from your law school studies, but they are not activities that you choose to partake of. The good and the bad distractions are those types of diversions that you consciously choose to participate in. You take the time to work out or watch a movie, for example. These distractions are not necessary to your livelihood, but are rather important to your sanity. Necessary distractions may be the most important type of distraction, as they keep you healthy and provide you with the essence of life, whether it is food, sleep, medicine, or anything and everything in between. Good distractions pull you away from law school and rejuvenate your mind, while necessary distractions maintain your physical health and nourish your body.

Take a look at the checklist below to ensure you are taking the proper necessary distractions and maintaining your life outside of law school:

- ❒ Doctor appointments
- ❒ Dentist appointments
- ❒ Grocery shopping
- ❒ Daily meals
- ❒ Snacks
- ❒ Hydration
- ❒ Family members
- ❒ Friends
- ❒ Sleep
- ❒ Human interaction
- ❒ Fresh air
- ❒ Relaxation
- ❒ Changes of scenery
- ❒ Vitamins
- ❒ Filling medicine prescriptions
- ❒ Pets
- ❒ Bills
- ❒ Cleaning
- ❒ Personal hygiene

Each of these necessary distractions provides a release from the stress of law school. They pull you away from your studies and allow you the opportunity to take care of your health and other responsibilities. Law school will inevitably take up a large amount of your time, but you simply cannot forsake the other parts of your life for it. Sure, you will have to scale back your time with your family and friends, and even walk Fido a little less, but these necessary distractions are all responsibilities present in your life before you entered law school.

It may sound silly, but eating healthy during law school and taking your vitamins will increase your ability to succeed. Most chapters in the book deal with studying or exam preparation. However, this chapter is unique as it focuses on increasing your ability to take the necessary steps to succeed. If you aren't healthy, you cannot study hard and you will not be able to focus on your course material. If you are distracted because you miss your friends and family, you will not be able to tackle a tough concept the week before the big test. These necessary distractions allow you to focus and give you the ability to succeed. Never underestimate the value of necessary distractions as they take time away from your studies on the front end, but they will save you time on the back end when it counts most. For example, by taking the time to go to the doctor when you feel ill, you can avoid a severe cold or get antibiotics to cure your ailments; or by shutting things down a few hours early and getting a good night's sleep you may keep from having to stop work during the day and take an unnecessary nap.

When the Stress Comes Marching In

Although you may take full advantage of your distractions and take time off from your studies, it is inevitable that at some point during your first year, you will be stressed out. Dealing with stress is just as important as avoiding stress to begin with. Stress can often seem like a black hole of sorts, as the harder you try to avoid it and get out of it, the farther into it you will find yourself. Feeling stressed out or burned out can occur at any point in the semester. The goal of this chapter is to enable you, as a first-year law student, to avoid a burnout. However, this section focuses on what exactly you should do if you take time away from law school and use those good distractions, but nevertheless find yourself stressed out.

Always remember that stress is a state of mind. You choose to be stressed out. If you allow yourself to remain calm and relaxed, you will not be stressed. You choose your own state of mind every day of your life. You decide if today will be a happy day or a sad one, just like you decide if today will be a stressful day or a manageable and calm experience. Half the battle with stress is how you deal with it when it hits you. Do you panic and shut down? Do you take a break and try to refocus your efforts? Do you let it overwhelm you to the point of personal destruction? These are the questions to answer through your actions. Stress is inevitable and unavoidable during your first year. However, how you deal with stress is completely up to you. You may have little control over the factors in your life that stress you out, but you have 100 percent of the control when you choose to react to those factors.

Take a few moments and look through this list of helpful actions and reactions you should have when and if stress comes marching into your life:

Talk to Your Professors

I have said it many times throughout this book and I will say it one last time: Professors are your allies and want nothing more than for you to succeed. Your success is a reflection of their teachings and your school's curriculum. The last thing anyone wants is to increase the dropout percentage. A great place to start when you feel stressed is to approach your professors and discuss your feelings. More times than not they will help you see the forest through the trees. Professors will help you to take a step away from the law school assembly line and gain a more insightful and relaxed perspective. Law school is not the end of the world and should not be viewed as such. It is merely a process of which you are a part, and it is one that you will survive; in the end, you will succeed. Talk to your professors, as they have been exactly where you are and know exactly how to deal with the stress.

Talk to Your Family and Friends

It is amazing the effect a little loving and kindness can have upon your stress levels. Sometimes everyone but you knows you will succeed, and just hearing that people believe in you will relax your nerves and reduce your stress levels. Take some time off and visit with your friends and family. They care for you, love you, and understand what you are going through, and most of them have experienced something similar during their own lives. Hearing their perspectives and opinions may allow you to take a good look at your situation and rethink your stress levels and refocus your energy.

Get the Work Done

There are many ways to control stress. A great way to reduce tension is to actually attack your stress. If you are stressed out about a paper, then do the paper. Complete the work, get it done, and get it out of the way. Most stress occurs because people put their energy into the stress and take their energy away from the actual work that is the source of the stress. Flipping out for an hour about a paper due the next day does nothing except take away an hour of valuable time to work on that paper. Focus on the work and it will instantly reduce the pressure you feel. Remember that feeling stressed out is a decision, and since you have ultimate control over what you decide to do, choose the work, not the stress.

Take a Break

I included an entire chapter in this book about distractions because they are one of the most important pieces of the law school success equation. It is no mystery that you need to relax to focus. If you are stressed and frustrated, you will not succeed. Sometimes the best thing you can do is step away from the work and focus on a distraction. I cannot stress it enough: Do not let yourself get to the point of unmanageable stress. Take those necessary breaks when you need them and you will greatly reduce your chances of burning out.

Keep Things in Perspective

Let's be honest here for a second. I am not an advocate for taking this view as your motto, but it is important to look at the consequences. Why are you ultimately stressed out? Most likely, you are anxious because you are scared of failure. You have been a success your entire life and you are so challenged at this point that you fear for the first time in your life you won't get the job done. So the worst thing that could happen is that you fail out of law school. Did someone die? No. Do you still have your health? Yes. Are you any less successful and intelligent now? No. You are the same person you were before law school, except now you learned a valuable lesson. That lesson is that law school and the legal field are not for you. Bill Gates. Donald Trump. Michael Jordan. Oprah Winfrey. The list goes on. These successful and famous people have one thing in common: They all failed at one point. They all struggled and they have all been challenged. However, they never gave up and they always maintained their focus. I will keep the pep talk short, but never forget that just getting into law school makes you a success. You beat out thousands of applicants to get where you are now. And if you fail, so what? Pick yourself back up and realize the world is still spinning and you will find the right place for yourself.

Stress is a part of the law school puzzle. Just like solving a Rubik's cube, solving the stress puzzle may take many different tactics and combinations, and relentless diligence. However, the point is that it is very manageable and very controllable if you relax and do not get to the point of total burnout. If you frantically move a Rubik's cube every which way, you will wear yourself out after little progress. The same is true with law school. If you frantically move about through law school with constant stress and little distraction and break from this tension, you will accomplish nothing and make the road to success an almost unnavigable one. However, if you focus your efforts and systematically approach law school, focusing on taking regular breaks and dealing with stress positively when it rears its ugly head, you will be fine, you will succeed, and you will not burn yourself out.

Fifteen-Minute Motivators

We have covered a lot of information in this chapter and I have tried to present every distraction imaginable and classify those distractions in a three-part system, focusing on those distractions that are good, those that are bad, and those that are necessary. It should be obvious at this point in your reading what the differences are between the three types of distractions and where you should spend your free time. Furthermore, it should be no surprise that if used correctly, distractions are not only a wonderful equalizer in the trials and tribulations of your first year, but will also help you navigate your road to success. No successful law student stayed in a library for four months straight. The human mind was not meant to be used without a break. You don't exercise until you black out. You don't shop until you run out of money. And you certainly don't study until you are burned out.

I am no David Letterman, but I have compiled a 1L "top-ten" list of what I like to call "fifteen-minute motivators." These are all distractions that can be completed in fifteen minutes or less and will ultimately give you the most bang for your buck, taking you away from law school and refreshing your mind and body. If you only have fifteen minutes and are feeling a little stressed, a little unnerved, and a little burned out, take one of these fifteen-minute breaks and then hit the books rejuvenated and relaxed as ever. Oh yeah, and in the spirit of calling my own shots, there are a whole lot more than ten of them. Catch me if you can, Dave.

- Make a phone call to a friend
- Take a walk outside
- Surf the Web (no Westlaw or LexisNexis—these don't count)
- Eat a snack
- Drink a cup of coffee
- Take a quick catnap
- Read a book (no law school books allowed)
- Watch some television
- Take your dog for a walk
- Do some sit-ups and pushups
- Jump rope
- Meditate
- Do some yoga
- Do Pilates
- Talk to a classmate
- Listen to music
- Download MP3s
- Burn a CD
- Do some online shopping (like window-shopping from your computer)
- Catch up on your e-mails
- Organize your schedule

- Take a shower
- Do breathing exercises
- Create a to-do list
- Plan a trip
- Pick a flower
- Make your bed
- Write in your journal
- Do your laundry
- Read the newspaper
- Read a magazine

This is an extensive list and you should be able to easily find a fifteen-minute motivator that is right for you. I generally work hard for an hour and then take a fifteen-minute break, as it keeps me fresh and motivated, allowing my mind to stay alert for longer study sessions. Always remember that Rome was not built in a day and you will not learn everything there is to know about property or contracts in one sitting. Use your time wisely, take breaks when necessary, and never forget the importance of a good ol' distraction.

MAY 15, 2003

School Is Out for the Summer

As I look at the clock, I know I am down to my last few minutes of my first year. If I can focus for just ten more minutes, I will walk out of this room as a second-year law student. I did it; I succeeded. I experienced the most challenging academic year of my life and in just a few minutes, I will have lived to tell about it. As I answer the last question on the exam with the few minutes I have left, I can't help but reminisce about my headaches, obstacles, and experiences. I truly can say that I have grown more in the past year than I did in the previous ten. After college I thought I knew everything, but after my first day of law school, it was obvious I really had the most important lessons still to learn. I meticulously browse through my exam to make sure I answered all of the questions, as if it would make any difference with two minutes left. I hear the proctor yell out "time," and I put my pencil down and look up as if I really have a clue what is going on at that very moment. I pull myself up from my seat, still sticking to it because of my sweat-inducing anxiety, and turn in my test. I take a deep breath of relief and briskly walk out of the exam room, noticeably more bouncy than when I walked in. I grab a drink, use the restroom, and begin walking to my car. I am overwhelmed by a feeling that has been missing from my life for almost a year:

pure, unadulterated relief. I don't even know where to begin. Should I go see a movie? Should I go work out? Should I just go to bed? As I am thinking about these perplexing and complicated issues in my life, I bump into my buddy and he looks at me quickly and says, "Man . . . I can't believe we are done. I guess the next thing is to figure out where we are going to work this summer." His words hit me like an ice-cold shower after a long sleep. What are we going to do this summer? And I thought I could take my first breath in a year. Here we go again. . . .

While congratulations are in order for finishing your last exam of your first year, do not lose sight of the ultimate goal: to leave law school with a great job. Job hunting began the moment you walked through the pearly gates of your law school and into that first classroom. From networking everyone you meet to obtaining good grades during your first year, all of these are parts of the equation for finding a good job. Finding this perfect job is not easy, and it may take you multiple experiences to find the right job for you. Whatever the case may be, remember that you are testing the water and learning from each of these experiences. For example, let's say you decide early on in law school you want to be a criminal defense attorney. You begin interviewing and networking with criminal defense attorneys across the city. You eventually find gainful employment with an attorney for the summer after your first year. After working half the summer, you realize this is not for you. That is okay. Finish your commitment, thank the attorney for the experience, and move on. It is a lot easier to spend a summer doing something you don't want to do than it is to spend your life doing something you don't enjoy.

I cannot stress enough the importance of clerking for a law firm after your first year. Even if it is part-time, unpaid, and extremely boring, the mere fact that you are getting meaningful law experience and building your resume is immeasurable. Along with studying hard during you first year, your other priority should be to set up some sort of clerkship for the summer. While you will be ahead of the game if you start early, do not fret if the summer starts without a job. Focus your time and effort on finding a position with an attorney in the area of law in which you are interested. You will be surprised how many attorneys are happy to offer you unpaid work. The mere fact that you can use Westlaw and LexisNexis is extremely valuable to them and if you get nothing out of the clerkship other than a recommendation letter, you are still ahead of the curve.

INsider's Guide

Attorney Advice

Attorney Justin Goodman says, "Summer clerkships are very necessary. Don't try to get the highest-paying one; try to get the one that will give you experience in something you might want to do with your career. If you try it out for the summer and do not like it, at least you know that area of law is not right for you. The worst thing you can do is sit around and do nothing all summer. This is a time to build your resume, network with attorneys, and gain some meaningful experience in the real world—because the real law world is a lot different than the one that you read about in books."

The Job Search

So you are probably lying in your bed or sitting on your favorite couch reading this book and thinking to yourself, "Okay, I get it. I need to find a summer clerkship, but I don't really know where to begin." While the last section should have planted the seed in your head that you need to have some type of clerkship during your summer breaks, this section is going to water that seed and watch it grow. I am going to walk you through the most helpful and beneficial ways of obtaining employment starting from your first class during your first year.

Career Services Office

Your career services office is a wonderful resource to use for finding summer clerkships and job listings. Their sole responsibility is to find you employment and they will diligently work with you and for you to build your resume and find you a summer clerkship. Most schools offer resume drops offs and adviser meetings early in the semester to create files for you and begin working for you. Take advantage of these early opportunities to get a jump-start on your first summer clerkship. More times than not, your career services office will have a limited number of jobs to work with, so getting an early jump on the available clerkships will only increase your chances of finding the right one for you. During orientation, visit the career services office to introduce yourself to the advisers and set up a meeting for the first week of school. The ultimate goal of law school is to leave with a job, so the earlier you start, the better chance you will have of achieving this end.

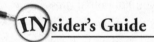

INsider's Guide

Student Counsel

3L Stacey Hornsby says, "Summer clerkships are a must. You have to do them. This is your chance to get your foot in the door to get a job offer upon graduation. Even if you don't want to work for the same firm you clerk for, do a great job. The references will go a long way, and future employers like to see firm work and clerkships on your resume. The summer is not the time to take off; you can use spring break for that."

Family and Friends

As discussed in the chapter on networking, friends and family are a wonderful way to gain job experience. Almost all of my summer clerkships were found through a family member or friend. If you are an in-state law student, you have a considerable advantage here because your family will certainly know an attorney or two in the city. If you are an out-of-state student, consider going home for the summer and working for a family friend or an attorney you know. It is extremely important to practice where you plan on playing, so if you plan on staying in the city where you are attending law school, try to gain employment there. Whatever the case may be, your family and friends will know attorneys, and if you probe enough, you might find yourself interviewing with a close friend of your family. Whatever the case may be, this is an easy and valuable resource to use when searching for summer clerkships, as this is an opportunity to get your family and friends to go to work for you and find you useful contacts.

Job Fairs

Job fairs are usually offered through your law school once or twice a semester. These are wonderful opportunities to network and find summer clerkships in a short period of time. The great thing about job fairs is that there are numerous clerkships in the same place. In just a short period of time, you can get your resume into the hands of ten to twenty employers, depending on the number of participants. The trick to gaining summer employment is in the numbers. If you apply to enough places, you will gain employment. Never put your eggs in one basket and always take advantage of job fairs, because they offer you a quick and effective way to find a clerkship.

Online Resources

Online resources and Web sites are a great way to search for clerkship opportunities. Whether it is an online employment Web site such as *www.Monster.com*, a local job-posting site, or your career services office Web site, these are great ways to network and apply for jobs. The best part is you can do it from the comfort of your own home. I would suggest that you visit these Web sites and post your resume, but do so on the weekends or at night, as this resource is open 24-7, while many of the other resources mentioned may not be available to you on the weekends or at night. Furthermore, most newspapers in big cities now have their own online resource for job searching and job posting, allowing you another resource to use when searching for summer clerkships.

Professors

Professors are awesome resources for two reasons. The first is that they themselves often need summer clerks and interns to help them with their own work, whether it be editing a law review article or researching for briefs and memos they are writing. They are always busy working on something for the upcoming school year and can always use help. Sometimes your school will even pay you and offer you class credit, along with the experience you are gaining by working with your professors. Secondly, professors can provide you with valuable networking opportunities with their colleagues. Most of your professors will have previously practiced law for a number of years, many of them at large law firms. Because of their experience, they will know an amazing number of people in the industry and can put you in touch with potential employers. Furthermore, many employers will call your professors to ask them if they have a student looking for some extra work or experience. Take a few minutes at the beginning of the semester and tell your professors what you are interested in. If they hear of any employment opportunities, they will almost certainly help you out in one way or another.

Previous Employers

Previous employers are a great place to start your first-year job search. Perhaps you interned for an attorney before law school or you shadowed an attorney in college before deciding to attend law school. Whatever the case may be, previous employers are always willing to give you a job or help you find employment if they were satisfied with your previous work. They know what you are capable of and already have a comfort level with you, so they are willing to invest their time and effort in helping you.

The Yellow Pages

This is pretty much like cold-calling. Go through the yellow pages and turn to the section on attorneys. Look through the names and descriptions and see if you can find a law firm or attorney that interests you. If you find one, do your background research on the attorney and give her a ring or send her an e-mail. Let her know that you are a first-year student looking for summer experience. You never know when you will catch an attorney overwhelmed with work and willing to offer you experience and an opportunity to make a little extra money. Here, you are simply playing your odds and if you call enough people, someone is bound to need some help. Even if it is unpaid, the fact that you are working at a law firm will put you ahead of your classmates who are taking the summer off to recover.

Prosecutor's and Solicitor's Offices

Many times, governmental offices such as the prosecutor's and solicitor's offices are dying for help. You may be a gopher and go for this and go for that, but just meeting the district attorneys and learning how the offices work will provide you with an advantage over your competition when you get out of law school and are ready to look for a job. Each office should be listed online and they are easy to find at your local courthouses. When you visit these offices, dress the part and take along a cover letter and a resume. Ask around to see if they need any help for the upcoming summer. You never know what you will find unless you step up to the plate and ask.

Nonprofit Organizations

Nonprofit organizations can be a slam-dunk for summer clerkships because they always need help. You obviously won't make any money, but this will quickly build your resume and even add a bit of humanitarianism to it. The wonderful part of working for these organizations is that they are always understaffed and are therefore willing to give you more responsibility than most other law firms.

I remember speaking to my fellow second-years who worked for nonprofits after their first year and many of them were fortunate enough to write memos and briefs, attend hearings, and interview clients, while I was dropping off briefs and getting clients coffee or a bottle of water.

Recruiters

Recruiters are probably one of the most underused resources by first-year law students. Most midsize to large law firms hire an individual solely for recruiting their new class of lawyers. This person is a gatekeeper of sorts and has huge pull when it comes to hiring. All of these recruiters will be listed online at the firm's Web site and are only an e-mail or phone call away. There is no harm in sending the recruiter an e-mail introducing yourself, with your resume attached. Who knows if the law firm needs a little pro bono help for the upcoming summer.

While all of these resources are unique, they do have one very important underlying concept in common: They all require you to proactively pursue them. In fact, this should be your motto for gaining meaningful employment after your first year and throughout your entire legal education. Proactive pursuit leads to jobs. No one will do it for you. You have to actively go after what you want, and if you chip away at it enough and call enough people, someone will come through and you will find exactly what you want.

Interviewing

If you effectively use the resources we have discussed, you will almost certainly have the opportunity to interview with a prospective employer. The interview process is as important as it comes. If your grades aren't great and your resume is a little empty but you have a great interview and wow your interviewer, there is a good chance you will get the job. I wasn't in the top 10 percent of my law school, but I was always prepared when interviewing and always had something to say. I impressed with my interviews and my character, which compensated for my grades. Once you have gotten your foot in the door, the job is yours to lose. Seriously, the hardest thing to do is to get employers to meet with you. If they do that, then they are somewhat willing to give you a shot, as they wouldn't waste time with an applicant they do not already like. That being said, once you get your foot in the door, take advantage of this wonderful opportunity to get a shot at a summer clerkship.

Interviewing is not brain surgery. Rather, it is just like your everyday interactions with your friends, family, and loved ones. I always like to look at an interview like a trip to the neighborhood grocery store. As you work your way through the store, you bump into an old friend and begin chatting with him about his life. You didn't plan on seeing him, but nonetheless, you ask him questions about himself and gain a better understanding of what has been going on in his life. You then go to checkout and talk to the cashier. You ask her how her day is going, what time she gets off, and if she watched the president speak last night. Finally, you strike up a conversation with the bag boy about his day. You ask him if he had a nice weekend and if he watched the high school football game last night. He says he plays on the team and you talk about his hopes and desire to play college ball. You thank him and drive off in your car.

During these exchanges, you did one thing. You communicated with each person and asked questions and responded to inquiries. You interviewed these people and they interviewed you. That is all an interview is. It is nothing to get worked up over and nothing to get excited about; it is simply a trip to the grocery store and a nice conversation with everyone you see there.

Important Interview Steps to Take

Dress the part. As previously mentioned, always dress up for an interview, because it expresses respect and preparation. Always dress professionally and look like you belong in the law firm. Underdressing can be an interview killer and get you a quick path to the exit.

Do your research. As obvious as it may seem, do your research on the law firm and the attorney with whom you are meeting. Where did the attorney go to college and law school? What are her main areas of practice? Where was she born? These are easy questions that you should already know the answer to before the interview.

Be on time. Better yet, be early. You should always be waiting on the attorney rather than the attorney waiting on you. I have seen attorneys tell students to go home if they were even a minute late. What if you were about to argue in front of the Supreme Court and you showed up late? Imagine every interview as the biggest case you will ever argue. Would you be late for that? Probably not. Get good directions and leave early so as to avoid being late and ruining your interview before it even begins.

Make a connection. Now that you are actually in the interview, always try your hardest to make a connection with your interviewing attorney. Take a look around her office and start there. Look at the pictures on the wall and the photos on her desk. Does she have a family? Does she love sports? Is she a movie buff? Who knows—any and all of these simple observations can give away valuable information and start conversations about something you are both interested in. Make as many connections as you can with your interviewer, as you never know what will be the one thing that sells this attorney on the fact that you are perfect for the job.

During my last year of law school I interviewed with an extremely well known and successful superior court judge, and I was one of many applicants. When I walked into his clerk's office, I noticed he had sports memorabilia all over the office. This was fortunate for me because I am a huge sports fan. I noticed he went to University of Georgia for undergrad and it just so happened their football team won a huge game the night before. I asked him if he watched the game and we spoke for twenty minutes about the game. We then ended the interview by reviewing my resume for five minutes. Two days later I got a call from the clerk saying that I got the internship. Who knows why I got it? Whatever the reason, I know that the mere fact that this clerk spoke about football for twenty minutes in the middle of his hectic day made him happy. I was also qualified for the internship, which helped, but I believe the mere fact that we had a common interest put me over the top.

Talk about yourself. In addition to making a connection, an interview is your opportunity to sell yourself. Don't sell yourself short. You are a success and you have accomplished some great things to be sitting in front of an attorney after your first year of law school. Talk about your accomplishments in a respectful and humble manner and illustrate your strengths and why you would be an asset to the law firm.

Have fun. Look, the bottom line is that if you are racked with nerves and anxiety, you will not interview well and you will not showcase your brilliant personality. I always viewed interviews as a fun opportunity to meet other people and simply chat with them about something that I really want to do. Sure, I wish I could do it in jeans and a T-shirt with a cup of coffee in my hand, but we can't have everything we want. Have a good time at interviews and enjoy yourself, because if you do, your interviewer will enjoy you more and have a better impression of your character.

Be professional. I know a lot of people who enter interviews and talk to the interviewer as if they are old buddies. The bottom line is that most interviewers will be younger, as there is no way a partner will take valuable time to interview an unpaid summer clerk. Because of this, many students think they can shoot the breeze and act laid back. I have always felt you should treat interviewers as if they are clients. Respectfully, regionally, and consciously. Be polite and address them by their proper title. I know they may be young, but you have to exude your professionalism and your dedication to the job you are interviewing for, regardless of their actions or tone.

Follow up. Lastly, always follow up after an interview and ask if there is anything further you need to do. Thank your interviewer promptly and tell her that you look forward to hearing from her in the near future. Showing you are excited about a job and interested in an opportunity can often be the difference between getting the clerkship and not. Being polite and creating an open line of communication between you and the interviewer is a highly effective way of gaining employment and even gaining a mentor or friend.

I Got the Job, Now What?

All right, so the interview went well and you got a summer job offer. Congratulations are in order, but don't pat yourself on the back for too long because now it is time to take advantage of your newest opportunity. Getting your foot in the door is the first step, but these opportunities will only be as successful and helpful to your future as you make them. If you impress your summer employers, there is a good chance you may receive another summer clerkship and eventually a job offer from them. If they cannot offer you another summer clerkship but are impressed with your work, they will almost certainly help you in any way that they can.

Valuable Tools for Your Summer Clerkship

See all you can see. During your time at your clerkship, you will see a lot of different things. One day you might be meeting with your boss and a client, the next running over to the courthouse and dropping off a brief. Take advantage of these opportunities and see all you can see. When you go to the courtroom, walk around for a few minutes and take a look behind a few doors (assuming you are allowed to open those doors). There is great value in familiarizing yourself with the courtrooms of your city and the surrounding buildings. You will inevitably spend a great deal of time in the courthouses as an attorney and a clerk, so knowing where they are and how they operate can be a highly effective tool. Furthermore, try to get involved with all the different happenings around the office. Express your desire to work with other attorneys and sit in on their meetings. Most law firms will have numerous attorneys practicing in many different areas of law, and you should take advantage of this and try to spend some time with each of them.

Meet your neighbors. Working in a law firm will give you a wonderful opportunity to meet numerous attorneys. All around the office you will find new opportunities and experiences. You will bump into attorneys in the mailroom, the copy room, the bathroom, and every other room in between. Strike up a conversation and introduce yourself. The more attorneys you meet, the better. When they are hiring from their summer clerks, you will be a step ahead of the competition if all the attorneys know you by name and can speak about your character and work ethic. Don't limit yourself because you are working with only one of the attorneys in the law firm. Meet with as many as you can, as each is a valuable resource for your job search and future.

Participate. Don't wait for the office to come to you; participate in the activities happening around you. Is there a deposition about to begin in the afternoon? An arbitration hearing in the morning? How about an interview with a new client over lunch? All of these unique experiences provide you with an opportunity to see something new and participate in it. Just looking on and taking it all in will inevitably help your understanding of the situation. Watch a deposition and you will quickly learn how to depose a witness. Interview a new client and you will know how to interact with your potential clients in the future. More often than not, your attorney will be extremely busy and unable to hold your hand each day. Be proactive and voice your desire to see all you can see and participate in whatever may present itself. This is your clerkship, so make the most of it and enjoy your time there.

Ask questions. Don't be shy; ask questions. With all of your new daily experiences, it is almost inevitable that you will see things you don't understand and participate in opportunities that render you clueless. However, your surrounding colleagues will have all of the answers. Ask them questions and show a desire to learn from these experiences. No one but you will know when you are confused, so step up to the plate and speak up when you need clarification. This also goes for all assignments you have. If you are writing a memo and do not understand how to create a persuasive fact pattern, ask your attorney how to do so. She will be much more responsive to clarifying a task than having to repeat it because you didn't know what you were doing from the beginning.

Express your gratitude. Frankly, wear your gratitude and your desire to be there on your sleeve. Always smile, always be polite, and always be overly energetic. People will respond to you if you exude the type of excitement that lets them clearly know you want to be there working for them. They will be more responsive to your questions, more caring about your experiences, and more willing to offer you a job for the next summer. Offer to take your boss out to lunch to get to know him better and thank him for the opportunity. Never underestimate the power of gratitude, as it reflects your desire to do what you are doing, which in turn makes people feel like they made the right decision by extending an offer to you.

Your first-year clerkship is a great opportunity to get your feet wet and find your niche in the legal community. If nothing else, make sure that before you leave your summer clerkship you get a recommendation letter from your boss to use in the upcoming year for job applications. It is often hard to track down attorneys, as they are awfully busy, so when you have the face time, use it to grab that valuable recommendation letter. Having references and support from the legal community will be helpful in the year to come. Furthermore, if you have the time, try to stay on and work part-time during the school year if you feel doing so would be a valuable experience. Showing longevity and dedication to a law firm illustrates that you are reliable and creates a better opportunity to lead to a job offer for your second year. Summer clerkships build off one another and one good performance can often lead to the opportunity to perform again. Always remember that school comes first and if your job will create stress and disable you from succeeding as a student, you should really reconsider working during the year. Whatever the case may be, getting your foot in the door for your first summer was a huge step and a big success, so pat yourself on the back and gear up for the upcoming year.

Back to School, Back to School

So the summer has come and gone and you are sitting in front of your computer a few days before school begins updating your resume and filling in the blanks. You had a successful summer and gained some great experience for your legal career. You go out one last time, have a nice evening with your friends, and begin getting ready for your first day of school. It seems like just yesterday you were sitting in orientation, freaking out about the impending first year.

Your second year will be a completely different experience than your first year for a few reasons. First, this is no longer a novel and unique experience to you. You know what to expect, you know how to handle the workload, and you are a year stronger and a year wiser. Half the shock of the first year of law school is the newness of the situation. Law school is unlike any academic experience you have ever had and the mere fact that you have to adjust to the experience is stressful enough. With your second year, there is no adjustment—just refocusing and staying the course.

Secondly, your second year is often easier because you are choosing your classes and can focus on those subjects that are interesting to you and your future. The mere fact that you are interested in something makes it an easier experience.

Thirdly, second-year classes offer you more options in the form of grades. Teachers are more willing to offer students take-home exams, open-book exams, and papers instead of the stressful in-class, closed-book exams from your first year. In fact, after my first year, I think I saw an in-class, closed-book exam only one time. The fact that you have the opportunity to choose the test format before you register for the class is valuable. For example, if you feel you perform best on take-home exams, read the course syllabi before registering and choose those classes offering take-home exams. I am an advocate for taking those classes that are useful to your future and will help you grow and learn, so do not take a class you have no interest in merely for the test format.

Preparing for your second year and managing your everyday tasks are similar to how you dealt with your first year. Prepare for your classes, study hard, and listen to your professors. They often say they scare you to death in the first year, work you to death in the second year, and bore you to death in the third year. I truly feel this little cliché is pretty accurate. During your second year, you won't be stressed because of the novelty of the situation, but rather you will be stressed because of the amount of work. In addition to fifteen hours of course work (for full-time students), you will most likely have papers to write and outside clerkships. During my second year, I worked for multiple law firms in addition to going to school and doing all of my work. Furthermore, you will be interviewing for summer clerkships and participating in clubs and other extracurricular activities. Your second year is the year to immerse yourself in the law school culture and focus on building your resume and gaining as many meaningful experiences as you possibly can.

While your second year may be just as challenging as your first year, it is definitely for different reasons. However, before your second year begins and you are once again caught up in the hustle of the game, focus your time and efforts on the following to make sure you are ready to play ball when you enter your first class of your 2L year.

Update your resume. While we haven't spoken a lot about your resume, I cannot stress the importance of having an orderly and updated resume. I have not given you a step-by-step process for creating a resume and updating it on a regular basis because I feel that is a step you should take on your own through your career services office. It will give you an opportunity to introduce yourself early and quickly get acquainted with the staff during your first semester at school. I will tell you this, though: Your resume is a reflection of your accomplishments and although it is only a piece of paper, it is the best argument you will have for why you should get the job. Your resume is your opportunity to shine and you should take full advantage of it. After creating your resume, send it to as many friends, attorneys, and proofreaders as possible to catch mistakes, edit your work, and ensure that you are putting your best foot forward. I have spoken to numerous hiring partners and recruiters and asked them how they deal with all the resumes they see and how they sort through them, and the most common statement is that they start by separating the resumes into two piles: those with spelling and grammatical mistakes, and those that are perfect. As you can imagine, one of those piles makes it through another read, while the other makes its way into the trashcan. So, take the time at the bare minimum to make sure your resume is mistake-free and ready to roll. This is your first impression, so make it a good one.

Pick some winners. Your second year is your first opportunity to actually choose the classes you would like to take. I always suggest covering the courses that will appear on the BAR. I know it seems like years away, but the BAR will sneak up on you, and it is great to have a working knowledge of all the BAR topics. You can always learn them in a review course, but it will only help you to be familiar with the subjects before you start the intensive course work. Furthermore, your second year is a time when you can take courses that interest you, whether they be criminal law courses or real estate courses, you can take your areas of interest and learn about them in detail. The nice part about your second year is that you are free to schedule courses at the times you find convenient. More often than not, your first-year courses are assigned for you and the times are not flexible. You may be stuck with all night classes or classes falling only in the morning. Your second year is a time for you to create a schedule you enjoy and can manage. If you want long weekends, you can avoid classes on Friday. If you want to work, you can avoid classes on certain days so you can clerk. Whatever it may be, pick classes for your second year to fit your schedule and your interests.

Interview, interview, interview. I cannot stress it enough that you should interview as much as you can before the school year actually begins. It is a lot more challenging to find time in your busy schedule to interview when you have classes to attend, cases to read, and papers to write. Use your downtime at the end of the summer to interview and set up a job for the upcoming school year, as it will take one responsibility off of your plate once everything else begins piling up. Always remember that there is power in numbers and the more interviews you go on, the more likely it is that you will succeed and find a job that will be right for you.

Recharge. All right, you finished your first year and then started working at a law firm. Take a few weeks before the semester begins to recharge and refresh. You have another long year ahead of you and you will need all of the energy and stamina that you can muster. You need to walk into that classroom ready to roll and ready to work hard for six months. I am a huge advocate for taking a long trip to the beach or visiting with friends and family before the rush begins. As you know by now, your free time will be reduced drastically once school begins, so take advantage of it while you have it.

Follow up with your summer clerkship. I always found it valuable when coming to the end of a summer clerkship to let my bosses know I would be happy to stay on throughout the year if they needed any help. This allows you to learn more and hopefully open up doors for a clerkship after your second year of law school. Offer to come in once or twice a week and be available if they need you in case of emergencies. There is no reason why you should not maintain a working relationship with your boss and keeps doors and communication lines open; you never know where they may lead.

After reading this section, you should now have a grasp of the steps you can take during the weeks before your second year to help you adjust and refocus for the challenge ahead. Your second year is really an interesting time in the law school journey, because you begin to get some real-world experience. You will inevitably spend just as much time in law offices and courtrooms as you do in class, providing you with unique and new opportunities to learn about the law and the legal community. The second year of law school was by far my favorite, as I had the chance to really expand my horizons and immerse myself in the legal world. I couldn't believe some of the experiences I was fortunate enough to have, and it really provided some relief from the everyday classroom experience. The second year is yours to enjoy and there is no reason why you should not have fun, gain some insight into your future, and prepare yourself for the final journey before you enter the real world.

The End (or Is It Just the Beginning?)
Wow, we have come a long way together, haven't we? From those first anxiety-inducing days in orientation to talking about summer clerkships, I have tried to cover every facet, challenge, and experience you will face during your first year. Ultimately, your law school journey and success will be a product of your dedication to the process. Law school is very systematic and success is in reach if you stay focused and work hard. No one will do it for you. This is your responsibility and your opportunity to grow and work toward what you want in life.

Your first year is just the beginning of the rest of your life, but it is also the foundation. Everything you experience and everything you participate in will be a byproduct of what you learned in your first year. Your core classes create an educational background that will serve you for the rest of your life. It is your choice how you decide to approach this foundation. However, I can tell you that the stronger the foundation, the bigger the house that rests on it can be. If you work hard, learn the materials, and seize your opportunities, you will be a great attorney. It all begins when you walk into that classroom on your first day. Every class you miss and every assignment you don't have time for makes a difference.

This is your life and this is your chance to prove you can get it done. In one fashion or another, everyone sees that sexy criminal case or that unbelievable products liability verdict and thinks in the back of their minds, "Man, it would be cool to a part of that." Trust me, you can be a part of that if you make the decision early in your first year to work hard and make it happen. Henry David Thoreau once said, "We are born to succeed, not to fail." This quote illustrates the underlying hopes of this book. This opportunity is yours to lose. You were born to succeed and you were wired to find success. You will find success in law school if you work hard and follow the resources and advice set forth in this book. Go forth, young scholar, and enjoy your journey, because you are lucky to be where you are. Good luck and keep up the hard work.

The Goods

This book has covered every piece of the law school puzzle, from the first day of orientation to the final minutes of your last first year exam. However, the resources and guidance do not end there. When you walk into your first law school classroom, or read through your first casebook, you will quickly find the language of the lawyers is significantly different than what you are probably used to. Use this final section as a quick reference guide for all of your law school terminology during your first year.

The Legalese

To succeed in any setting, you must excel and understand the terminology and language. Law school calls for the knowledge of a specific set of terms and language known as legalese. Legalese has many unique and different terms rarely used in normal English verbage along with certain terms that have a different meaning than what we commonly understand.

Use this legal dictionary from Wikipedia.com to familiarize yourself with legalese before your first year begins and also as a resource during your reading and research to clarify words you do not already understand:

Glossary of Legal Terms

A

Abet

To encourage or set another on to commit a crime. This word is always taken in a bad sense. To abet another to commit a murder, is to command, procure, or counsel him to commit it. Old Nat. Brev 21; Col Litt. 475.

Abettor

One who encourages or incites, persuades or sets another on to commit a crime. Such a person is either a principal or, an accessory to the crime. When present, aiding, where a felony is committed, he is guilty as principal in the second degree ; when absent, "he is merely an accessory." 1. Russell, 21; 1 Leach 66; Foster 428. Source: Bouvier's Law Dictionary, Sixth Edition, Revised, 1856.

Accessory

An accessory is one who knows of, and assists in, the commission of a crime, but is not present when the crime is committed. In this an accessory is different from an accomplice. A person may be an accessory either before or after the fact; that is, before or after the crime is actually committed. A person cannot be an accessory unless a crime is eventually committed.

Accomplice

Individual who voluntarily engages with another in the commission or attempted commission of a crime.

Acquittal

To be found not guilty of a violation of law.

Adversarial system

A system of justice in which advocates for opposing parties each do their best to present evidence and arguments to the benefit of their respective clients; presiding judges are neutral and passive. See Inquisitorial system.

Affidavit

Written statement of fact, signed and sworn to before a person having authority to administer an oath.

Arraignment

In criminal cases, a court hearing where the defendant is advised to the charges and asked to plead guilty or not guilty.

Appeal

Process by which a case is brought from one court to a higher court for review.

Alibi
A provable account of an individual's whereabouts at the time of the commission of a crime which would make it impossible or impractical to accuse the person.

C

Capital Offense
A criminal offense punishable by death.

Case-in-chief
That portion of a case in which the litigant has the burden of presenting evidence.

Change of venue
A change of venue is a legal term that means that a case before a court will be heard in another jurisdiction versus the one where the said crime took place. This is done when there is a reason to think that a defendant will not receive a fair trial, for whatever the reason.

Class Action
Lawsuit brought by a representative member(s) of a large group of people on behalf of all members.

Conviction
To be found by a judge or jury to have violated a law. Note that a conviction does not necessarily mean the person has committed a crime. A person who receives a parking ticket or a traffic ticket only punishable by a fine and is found guilty stands convicted of the charge even though traffic and parking offenses are not crimes.

Crime
A violation of law which is an offense against the state and generally punishable by some form of penalty which could include prison or jail time. Crimes are defined as serious felonies or less serious misdemeanors. A violation of law which only has a monetary penalty is not a crime per se, but an infraction.

Cross Examination
Questioning of a witness during a trial or during the taking of a deposition, by the party opposed to the one who produced the witness.

D

Deposition
Testimony taken under oath and recorded in an authorized place outside the courtroom.

De Minimis
Trifling or minimal; A fact or thing so insignificant that a court may overlook it in deciding an issue or case. Often misspelled de minimus.

Direct Appeal
A proceeding in which a convicted person asks a higher court to overturn a conviction or sentence received at the trial court based on alleged errors which appear in the trial record.

Direct Examination
Questioning of a witness in a trial, or at the taking of a deposition, by the party for whom the witness is testifying.

Dismissal
Termination of a legal proceeding prior to finding. A dismissal can be with or without prejudice.

E

Estoppel
A principle of equity whereby a person is not allowed (is, therefore, estopped) from maintaining or relying upon the existence of a certain state of affairs. It is often said to be a shield not a sword, i.e., to afford a defence to a claim rather than the basis for a claim, but in certain cases the effect of an estoppel is to confer actionable legal rights. If, for example, a promise is made which

is not legally enforceable because there has been no consideration provided for it, and it would be inequitable for the promise to be broken, the promisor may be estopped from reneging on the promise.

Exhibit

The paper, document, or other physical object received by the court as evidence during a trial.

Ex parte

By or for one party without notification of nor representation on behalf of other parties. A variant is ex parte on notice where the other party has received informal or short notice, but not formal or full notice. When an application is made ex parte the other side is not heard, and there is therefore an obligation of full and frank disclosure on the part of the applicant in order to present a fair picture to the Court being asked to make any decision.

Express authority

An employee who is hired by agreement (oral or written) is an agent and has been given express authority to act on behalf of the business. That authority, however, may be limited; an express contract specifies the limitations of an agent's authority.

F

Felony

A serious crime, which is punishable by imprisonment of at least one year, or by execution, or by fine or both fine and imprisonment. It is distinguished from a misdemeanor as the maximum imprisonment for a misdemeanor is less than one year.

Fixed-price contract

A contract which is framed in such a way that, when the contractor finishes the agreed-upon work, it will only receive the pre-arranged compensation, regardless of what their costs were. The compensation is usually based on the expected expense of completing the work, plus a pre-arranged amount, so that the contractor can earn a profit instead of breaking even. If the contractor is able to complete the work under-budget, those savings become extra profit. Going over-budget, however, reduces the amount of profit realized from the contract and may even result in the contract being a net financial loss, providing strong incentive to minimize expenses. This is in contrast to a cost-plus contract.

G

Grantee
A grantee is a person to whom something is granted. In a franchise agreement, for example, the party buying the franchise is the grantee.

Grantor
A grantor is a person who grants something (typically, rights or real property). In a franchise agreement, for example, the party selling the franchise is the grantor.

I

Inadmissible
That which under the established rules of evidence, cannot be admitted or received in court.

In Camera
In secret. A basic principle of justice is the court open to the public but at times, proceedings may be closed.

Indictment
Written accusation of a grand jury, charging that a person or business committed a crime.

Infraction
An essentially minor violation of law where the penalty upon conviction only consists of monetary forfeiture. A violation of law which could include imprisonment is a crime. It is distinguished from a misdemeanor or a felony in that the penalty for an infraction cannot include any imprisonment.

Injunction

Any court order prohibiting some parties from specific actions and/or activities (for example, working for a competitor in breach of duty to an existing employer) on penalty of contempt of court. It is, in exceptional cases, possible to obtain a mandatory injunction, which is a court order compelling a certain course of action (for example, demolition of an illegal structure) on penalty of contempt of court.

Inter Alia

"Among other things." Used in pleadings before a court or opinions of a court, such as, "The defendant claims, inter alia, that the plaintiff fails to establish . . ."

J

Jurisprudence

Theory and philosophy of law, which determines appropriate goals and methods of justice.

L

laches

An equitable defense accusing an opposing party of having "sat on its rights"; as a result of this delay, the delaying party is undeserving of equitable relief. It is a form of estoppel for delay.

Libel

An untrue statement published in print and communicated to a third party with the purpose to damage the reputation of another.

M

Mens Rea

Mens rea is the Latin term for "guilty mind" used in the criminal law. The standard common law test of criminal liability is usually expressed in the Latin phrase, *actus non facit reum nisi mens sit rea*, which means that "the act will not make a person guilty unless the mind is also guilty."

Miranda Rights
A list of rights that police in the United States must read to suspects in custody before questioning them, pursuant to the Supreme Court decision in Miranda v. Arizona.

Misdemeanor
A less serious crime which is punishable by a fine, by imprisonment of one year or less, or by both. Some jurisdictions classify all violations of law which are less than felonies as misdemeanors, however generally a violation of law which is only punishable by a fine, and which cannot be punished by imprisonment, is considered an infraction (and not a crime), rather than a misdemeanor.

Mistrial
Erroneous or invalid trial. Usually declared because of prejudicial error in the proceedings, hung jury, or when the proceedings must be interrupted.

Motions
Oral or written requests made by a party to an action and brought before a judge prior to, during, or after a trial.

O

Objection
Statement by an attorney in opposition to testimony, or the attempted admission of evidence, and opposing its consideration as evidence.

Offense
Any accusation of violation of law, whether it is a criminal violation (such as murder) or a non-criminal infraction (such as a parking ticket).

On the merits

Describes the ultimate decision or judgment of a case. A decision on the merits is a judgment based on the facts, rendered after a full presentation of the evidence has been heard, as opposed to one based on legal technicalities or procedural deficiencies.

P

Pardon

Legal release from the punishment of a crime.

Plea

A statement made by the defendant as to his/her guilt or innocence to the charge made against him or her.

Plea Bargain

The process by which the accused and the prosecutor negotiate a mutually satisfactory disposition of the case. Such bargains are not binding on the court.

Precedent

Judicial decision that serves as an example for how to rule in similar cases

Prejudice

The ability of a party whose case has been dismissed to refile it with the court, usually after overcoming the issue that led to its dismissal. If a case is dismissed with prejudice it may not be refiled; if it is dismissed without prejudice, the plaintiff (civil) or prosecutor (criminal) is permitted to refile if they so wish.

Prima facie

Latin for "At first sight." Self-evident; obvious. A prima facie case is where the plaintiff presents enough evidence to win outright barring any defenses or additional evidence presented by the defendant.

Pro hac vice

"For this occasion," application by an out-of-state lawyer to represent his or her client. Since lawyers are licensed by each state independently they must ask for permission of the court to appear in matters before any other state courts. Permission is generally granted though the details can vary from one jurisdiction to another.

R

Res Ipsa Loquitur

Latin for "the thing speaks for itself." In Torts, it is the doctrine providing that, in some circumstances, the mere fact of an accident's occurrence raises an inference of negligence so as to establish a prima facie case.

S

Slander

The tort of making false oral statements damaging to another person's reputation; the oral form of defamation.

(The) State

The body politic, the government. This meaning is indicated by the definite article—The State.

Subpoena

Coming from the Latin for "under penalty" (sub poena), a subpoena is a court process used to cause a witness to appear and give testimony, commanding him or her to appear before the court or magistrate therein named, at a time therein mentioned, to testify for the party named, under a penalty therein mentioned. This is formally called a subpoena ad testificandum, to differentiate it from a subpoena duces tecum, which refers to documents.

On proof of service of a subpoena upon the witness, and that he is material, a citation may be issued against him or her for contempt, or (conceivably) a bench warrant for his or her arrest may be issued, if he or she neglects to attend as commanded. The equivalent command to a defendant is a summons.

T

Tort

A civil wrong (as opposed to a criminal wrong), which may be either intentional or accidental. If someone is driving and hits an unoccupied parked car, they commit a tort in that they have caused a wrong to another party which does not rise to the level of a crime. If they fail to stop at the scene of the accident, they also commit a crime, which is a criminal wrong in addition to, and separate from the tort.

Tortfeasor

The title given to an actor who commits a tort.

U

Uphold

To maintain.

V

Venue

Neighborhood, neighboring place; synonymous with place of trial. It refers to the possible or proper place(s) for trial of a suit, as among several places where jurisdiction could be established.

Versus

Against or opposed to, the abbreviation v. usually used in case names (for example: McCulloch v. Maryland). In Commonwealth countries such as England and Australia, it is usually read as "and" in civil matters (Strickland v Rocla Concrete Pipes Ltd would be Strickland "and" Rocla Concrete Pipes Ltd) and "against" in criminal matters (Dietrich v The Queen would be Dietrich "against" The Queen).

Reference
"Glossary of legal terms," Wikipedia, The Free Encyclopedia, *http:// en.wikipedia.org/wiki/List_of_legal_terms* (accessed January 10, 2007).

Distractions, 159–83
  advantageous times for, 162–65
  after exams, 125–26
  alcohol as, 174
  alleviating, 23
  author experience, 159
  bad, 161, 172–76
  before bedtime, 163
  car analogy, 161
  between classes, 162–63
  drugs as, 174
  during exams, 163–64
  family and friends as, 169–70
  fifteen-minute motivators,
      182–83
  good, 160–61, 165–71
  during holidays, 164, 166
  importance of, 160, 181–82
  Internet as, 175
  during long study periods, 163
  meals as, 169
  movies as, 168
  necessary, 161, 176–78
  nightlife as, 173
  pervasiveness of, 162
  reading as, 171
  roommates as, 175–76
  shopping as, 170–71
  significant others as, 167–68
  stress and, 178–81
  television as, 23, 163, 170, 174,
      182
  trips as, 173
  types of, 160
  vacations as, 166–67, 173
  on weekends, 164–65
  during winter/spring breaks,
      164, 166–67
  workouts as, 169
  writing as, 171
Dog days, avoiding, 26–27
Drugs, 174

Editing
  allowing time for, 136
  assessing arguments, 155, 156

  at end, 155–56
  importance of, 132
  process, 147–48, 155–56
  resources for, 154–55
  undergraduate vs. 1L writing,
      132, 136
Etiquette
  in class, 32–34
  networking, 74–76
Examples and explanations
    (E and Es), 30–31
Exam preparation. *See also* Outlines
  CALI for, 108–9
  hypothesizing practice problems,
      107–8
  meeting with professors, 108
  networking during, 61
  night before exams, 110–11
  old exams for, 109
  online resources for, 108–9
  perspective on, 109–10
  planning ahead, 106–7
  process overview, 86–87
  reviewing outline for, 107
  reviewing with friends, 108
  scheduling and, 86–87
  summary, 127
  tips, 106–10
Exams
  aftermath of, 124–27
  author experience, 79, 105
  closed-book, closed-note, 83
  compared to undergrad exams,
      86–87
  congratulating yourself after, 127
  focusing on controllables, 81–82
  getting out of town after,
      125–26
  hiding study materials after,
      126–27
  in-class, 83–84
  intimidating nature of, 80, 82
  keeping perspective on, 124–25
  mental approach to, 80–82
  not talking with classmates after,
      125–26

old, reviewing, 41
open-book, open-note, 83–84
Professor Pointers on, 111, 116,
    122, 125
professors helping pass, 102–3
relaxing between, 126
scope of, 82–83
syllabi indicating structure of,
    102–3
take-home, 85–86
weight of, affecting grades,
    124–25
Exams, taking
accessories for, 113–14
in afternoon, 112
answering questions, 114–24,
    138
applying rule of law, 120–21
distractions during, 163–64
drawing conclusions, 122–23
fact patterns, 83, 115–16, 118,
    119–21, 123
first task, 114–15
IRAC process, 119–23
issue statements, 119–20
managing time, 116–17
in morning, 112
at night, 112–13
night before, 110–11
outlining answers, 117–19
overview, 110
Professor Pointers, 111, 116,
    122, 125
reading instructions/questions,
    114–15
reviewing answers, 123
rule of law determination, 120
starting times and, 111–13
what to bring, checklist, 113–14
writing more, not less, 123–24
writing skills and, 138

Fact patterns
exams, 83, 115–16, 118, 119–21,
    123

memos, 137
writing, 144, 197
Family
clerkships through, 188–89
helping with stress, 179
as positive distraction, 169–70
as professors, 52–53
Fifteen-minute motivators, 182–83
First day of school
author experience, 1–2
orientation preparing you for,
    2–5
in perspective, 5–6
syllabus day vs., 5
typical school day and, 6
Formatting writings, 145–46
Friends. *See also* Classmates
clerkships through, 188–89
distractions with, 170
helping with stress, 179
professors as, 52–53
significant others, 167–68

Glossary, 205–16

Holidays, 164, 166
Hypothesizing practice problems,
    107–8
Internet
as distraction, 23, 175
resources. *See* Online resources
Interviewing, for jobs, 192–95,
    201. *See also* Networking

IRAC process, 119–23

Job hunting. *See* Clerkships

Law organizations, 62
Legalese, 205
Legal writing, 129–57
adapting, to surroundings, 148–49
answering questions, 133
author experiences, 129–31

Justin Spizman is a recent graduate of The Georgia State University School of Law. To prepare for this book project, in his final semester as an undergraduate honor student at the University of Texas, Spizman authored an independent study exploring success in a student's first year of law school. Throughout his first two years of law school, Spizman clerked for criminal defense and entertainment attorneys to gain legal experience and training. Even though Spizman survived his first year, he realized how much he wished he had known before his first year began. During the first year of law school, Spizman kept a journal of his experiences and interviewed other first-year students and professors as well as leading attorneys to determine what first-year students must know to succeed. He authored this book during his third year of law school, where he also served as Vice President of the Sports and Entertainment Law Society and clerked for a prominent Judge in Fulton County.